REFRAMING TEACHER LEADERSHIP

TO IMPROVE YOUR SCHOOL

DOUGLAS B. REEVES

ASCD

Association for Supervision and Curriculum Development • Alexandria, Virginia USA

Association for Supervision and Curriculum Development
1703 N. Beauregard St. • Alexandria, VA 22311 1714 USA
Phone: 800-933-2723 or 703-578-9600 • Fax: 703-575-5400
Web site: www.ascd.org • E-mail: member@ascd.org
Author guidelines: www.ascd.org/write

Gene R. Carter, *Executive Director*; Nancy Modrak, *Publisher*; Julie Houtz, *Director of Book Editing &*
Production; Miriam Goldstein, *Project Manager*; Georgia Park, *Senior Graphic Designer*; Mike Kalyan,
Production Manager; Cynthia Stock, *Typesetter*; Carmen Yuhas, *Production Specialist*

Printed in the United States of America. Cover art copyright © 2008 by ASCD. ASCD publications present a variety of viewpoints. The views expressed or implied in this book should not be
interpreted as official positions of the Association.

All Web links in this book are correct as of the publication date below but may have become
inactive or otherwise modified since that time. If you notice a deactivated or changed link, please
e-mail books@ascd.org with the words "Link Update" in the subject line. In your message, please
specify the Web link, the book title, and the page number on which the link appears.

ASCD Member Book, No. FY08-7 (May 2008, P). ASCD Member Books mail to Premium (P) and
Comprehensive (C) members on this schedule: Jan., PC; Feb., P; Apr., PC; May, P; July, PC; Aug.,
P; Sept., PC; Nov., PC; Dec., P.

PAPERBACK ISBN-13: 978-1-4166-0666-6   ASCD product #108012

Also available as an e-book through ebrary, netLibrary, and many online booksellers (see Books in
Print for the ISBNs).

Quantity discounts for the paperback edition only: 10–49 copies, 10%; 50+ copies, 15%; for 1,000
or more copies, call 800-933-2723, ext. 5634, or 703-575-5634. For desk copies: member@ascd.org.

Library of Congress Cataloging-in-Publication Data

Reeves, Douglas B., 1953–
  Reframing teacher leadership to improve your school / Douglas B. Reeves.
     p. cm.
  Includes bibliographical references and index.
  ISBN 978-1-4166-0666-6 (pbk. : alk. paper)
  1. Teachers—Training of—United States. 2. Educational leadership—United States.
3. School improvement programs—United States. I. Title.

  LB1715.R345 2008
  371.1'06—dc22   2008000481

15 14 13 12 11 10 09 08   1 2 3 4 5 6 7 8 9 10 11 12

REFRAMING TEACHER LEADERSHIP

to Improve Your School

ASCD MEMBER BOOK

Many ASCD members received this book as a member benefit upon its initial release.

Learn more at: **www.ascd.org/memberbooks**

REFRAMING TEACHER LEADERSHIP
TO IMPROVE YOUR SCHOOL

Acknowledgments

Although each of my more than 20 books has been a collaborative affair, no project has involved more people with more intensive effort than *Reframing Teacher Leadership to Improve Your School*. My first and most important acknowledgments are to the educators and school leaders who voted with their hearts, minds, conscience, and feet, displaying their work, warts and all, to their colleagues, their local stakeholders, and now the world. You can find their names and action research projects in Appendix A, but such a listing fails to do justice to their intellectual energy and personal courage. If you want to see teacher leadership in action, my words take a distant second place to the daily actions of these classroom educators and school leaders.

Although the popular refrain among critics is to bewail central office administrative positions as a useless appendage unrelated to teaching and learning, we must occasionally let evidence intrude on prejudice. Karlene Lee, Arlene Lewis, Gwen Marchand, and their colleagues are walking evidence of the proposition that there is no contradiction between central office administration and deep and abiding care for students and teachers. I also wish to acknowledge the support and cooperation of Chief Academic Officer Lauren Kohut-Ross and Superintendent Walt Rulffes, along with the support of State Superintendent Keith Rheault and Public Education Foundation Chair Vaughna Bendickson.

Cathy Shulkin reviewed and edited every word of the manuscript, saving me a thousand times from embarrassment as I seek to translate ideas into words, sometimes forgetting that the reader may not understand that a change in flights does not excuse the omission of an explanatory transition.

My colleagues at the Leadership and Learning Center have been especially helpful in this project. In particular, I wish to acknowledge Laura Besser, Ramona Gonzales, and Robin Hoey for reviews of the quantitative and qualitative data; Larry Ainsworth, Elle Allison, Connie Kamm, Brian McNulty, and Stephen White for their intellectual inspiration; and Nan Caldwell, Peggy Lush, and Jason Mueller for their service to the participants in this project and exceptional attention to detail.

Every time I acknowledge my family's role in my research and work it is inadequate and late. As every parent knows, the distance from the first ultrasound image to the first college tuition payment is but the blink of an eye. As Julia heads to college, I will hold in my mind the image of the giggly kindergartner she was only moments ago. Her brothers, James and Alex, are young men of whom I am especially proud, not because of my influence but because of their choices of service, scholarship, and familial support. Brooks is on the path to becoming a teacher, making his father, grandfather, grandmother, and several previous generations of teachers prior to that burst with pride.

Douglas Reeves, Swampscott, Massachusetts

1

WHY A NEW FRAMEWORK FOR TEACHER LEADERSHIP?

One cannot read Plato's accounts of the dialogues of Socrates and believe that teacher leadership is a 21st century idea. From his first days in the Lyceum to the last drop of hemlock and his journey to the Elysian Fields, teacher and leader were one. Even though 21st century educators are fond of the new—and this book will not disappoint in that respect—contemporary authors are disingenuous if they fail to recognize the shoulders on which they stand. Names we know—Diderot, Kant, and Locke from Europe—and teachers whose identities we infer from archaeological records from Africa, Asia, and South America all testify to the truth that teaching and leadership are inseparable qualities. In the 21st century, influential scholars have advocated distributed leadership (Elmore, 2000), implying that hierarchy is less effective than networks (Reeves, 2006b). Whether the perspective is from ancient times, the Renaissance, the previous century, or tomorrow, teachers and school leaders continue to focus on an essential question: how can we transcend the boundaries among teachers, leaders, and political authorities in a way that allows us to nurture, challenge, encourage, and develop every student entrusted to our care? I will attempt to address that question in the following pages.

If teacher leadership is not a new concept, why am I proposing a new framework for teacher leadership? The straightforward, if immodest, response is that although the existing teacher leadership literature contains many compelling anecdotes and rhetorical flourishes, it is strikingly unburdened by evidence and systematic research. In the course of more than 2 million miles of travel to schools around the globe, I have learned at the very least that teachers and school leaders demand practical information and applicable research. The framework is based on a study of students, teachers, and school leaders from demographically, economically, and linguistically diverse areas. This study, supported by the Public Education Foundation of Clark County and the Clark County School District Office of Research and Accountability, included 81 schools in Clark County, Nevada, the United States' fourth-largest school system, with a student population of more than 330,000 pupils. Clark County is an ideal research environment because it includes urban, suburban, and rural schools with a wide range of student characteristics. Teams of teachers and school leaders from throughout the county applied for participation in the research project (see Appendix B for the research proposal form and Appendix C for the rubric used to evaluate the applications). Eighty-two applications were accepted, and 81 research teams completed the project. Research began in the fall of 2006 and was completed in the spring of 2007. Participating teams represent all grade levels, from prekindergarten through high school, and a wide range of subjects. Appendix A includes the abstracts for all of the projects.

Although many research conclusions are equivocal, the results of this study are clear and striking. Teachers not only exert significant influence on the performance of students, but they also influence the performance of other teachers and school leaders. Overall, the educators in this study reported that they were more likely to be influenced by the professional practices and action research of their peers than they were to be influenced by journal articles or undergraduate or graduate courses. With the response range including 1 (not influential); 2 (rarely influential); 3 (somewhat influential); and 4 (very influential), the average ratings were as follows: undergraduate courses, 1.8; professional reading, 2.3; graduate courses, 2.6; and advice from a colleague, 3.6.

When offered the opportunity to list all of the influences on their professional practices, these teachers emphasized other teachers, students, family, and personal experience over many other presumed influences on their practice. Figure 1.1 shows the percentage of total responses each source of influence received from participants.

Figure 1.1

Sources of Influence on Practice Indicated by Open Response

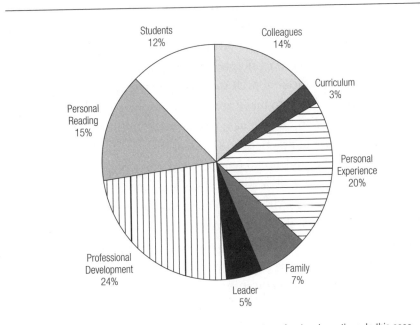

Respondents were allowed to list up to four influences on their professional practices. In this case, there were 86 respondents and thus a possible total of 344 sources of influence on professional practice. Each slice represents the percentage of the total possible responses.

The most important finding of the study—and the foundation of my New Framework for Teacher Leadership—is that direct observation of the professional practices of teachers by teachers must become the new foundation of professional development. This finding turns on its head much of the change-theory literature that presumes that system change is a top-down affair, dominated by a charismatic chief executive with an inspiring vision who, with a combination of persuasion and brute force, creates the buy-in necessary for systemic change, or at least the appearance of change until the expiration of the charismatic leader's contract. Although the evidence does not render professional development seminars irrelevant, it does place them within a broader perspective. Leaders at every level should compare their professional development calendar and budget to the relative impact of alternative sources of influence on teacher practice. The combined influence of professional development, leadership, and curriculum accounts for about one-third of the sources of influence identified by teachers on their practice.

Guskey (2000) and Sparks and Hirsch (1997) have long warned of the limitations of traditional professional development, and they have wisely counseled schools to make greater use of job-embedded professional development and to evaluate results based on the observable impact on professional practices and student results. The New Framework for Teacher Leadership takes this thoughtful advice to the next step by making action research by teachers and school leaders the heart of professional learning. Although some readers may regard this approach as little more than common sense, we must contrast common sense with common practice. In many school systems, professional development strategies continue to rely on a combination of outside experts' inspirational speeches and administrators' stern follow-up memos. Too rarely are educators asking the most fundamental question in education research: is it working?

From the standpoint of a professional developer, a person who spends a good deal of his life attempting to improve student achievement by improving the knowledge and skills of educators and leaders, it is some consolation that about 40 percent of the influence on teachers and leaders may be associated with the professional development seminars, books, and articles to which I have devoted my professional life. What about the other 60 percent? Let the data speak. Teachers and leaders are influenced by their own colleagues, their own experiences, their own students, and their familial associations. It is a conceit beyond words for educational leaders to say that training is equivalent to influencing professional practices.

The participants in this study are at the same time exceptional and ordinary. They are exceptional because they represent the best our profession has to offer—diligent, caring, and dedicated. But are their characteristics so different from those of teachers in school systems around the world? If this particular sample is truly exceptional, then the results of this research are unlikely to be replicated. If, on the other hand, we have a group of excellent educators who, in fact, are not out of the ordinary, then the results of the study are far more meaningful. Appendix A contains a list of participant names, their research questions, and abstracts of their findings. The teacher researchers in this study had an average of 13.7 years in the profession and 8.7 years with their current school systems. Of the educators participating, 68 percent had a master's degree, 16 percent held a bachelor's degree, 10 percent held a doctorate, and 6 percent had a specialist's degree. In terms of participants' job roles, 68 percent were classroom teachers, 16 percent were administrators, and the remaining participants had other duties, including coaching and counseling. Considering the composition of this sample, the research results are strongly biased in favor of working classroom professionals. These findings are not based on researchers who, on the side, do a little bit of teaching. Rather, the research in the following pages is based on teachers who, on top of their already busy schedules, have decided to engage in research.

The research questions considered include a wide spectrum of topics at the forefront of educators' and leaders' concerns. Studying students from prekindergarten through high school, research teams investigated questions about reading, writing, science, math, music, social studies, health, and physical education. The student populations included special education, English language learners, and economically disadvantaged students, as well as regular education, English-speaking students, and economically advantaged students. Schools from urban, suburban, and rural areas participated in the study. In addition to considering explicit academic subjects, researchers considered critical thinking, analysis, student engagement, attitudes, beliefs, and parent involvement. Several studies specifically addressed student behavior, and many other studies included observations about improvements in student behavior that occurred coincidentally with improvements in academic achievement.

Demographic Characteristics and Student Achievement: The Role of Leadership Attitudes

Student demographic characteristics clearly have an impact on student achievement (Rothstein, 2004a, 2004b). Every day, however, teachers must grapple with the weight demographic characteristics have compared with the weight their professional practices have. Few people would deny that housing, health care, nutrition, and home environment profoundly influence students' educational opportunities, but the central question is whether those influences render teacher professional practices impotent. The perceptions of teachers in this study suggest that teacher practice is not only important but also significantly greater in influencing student achievement than student demographic characteristics. Teachers were asked to respond to the following prompt: "If I were giving advice to a new superintendent or central office leader, the most important thing I would say is. . . ." The response range included 1 (strongly disagree); 2 (disagree); 3 (no opinion); 4 (agree); and 5 (strongly agree). The average ratings were as follows: student demographics, 3.21; leadership practices, 3.33; and teaching practices, 4.21. Note that teachers made these responses after conducting their own action research.

Are these perceptions simply the delusional views of a few Pollyannas? That is the stereotype cast by those who resolutely believe that teachers are, in essence, potted plants decorating a school with good intentions while demographic destiny marches onward. Given the extensive professional experience—an average of almost 14 years—and education of this sample, such a stereotype is hardly persuasive. But at the end of the day, it is evidence, not perception, that must carry the argument. In a study of the same 330 schools from which the current teacher research sample was drawn, the Leadership and Learning Center examined the extent to which school leadership teams attributed the causes of student achievement to student demographic characteristics or to teachers, and compared those perceptions with measurements of student achievement in reading, writing, math, science, and social studies on a variety of assessments. Specifically, the following assessments were considered: the Criterion-Referenced Test, the High School Proficiency Examination, the Iowa Tests of Basic Skills, the Iowa Tests of Educational Development, and the Nevada Analytic Writing Examination. Those results, originally reported in *The Learning Leader* (Reeves, 2006a), indicate that in schools where leadership teams primarily attributed student achievement to student demographic variables, an average of 43.6 percent of students scored proficient or higher on a group of 25 assessments. In contrast, in schools where leadership teams primarily attributed student achievement to faculty variables, an average of 64.8 percent of students scored proficient or higher on those assessments.

The findings are eerily reminiscent of the Pygmalion effect (Rosenthal & Jacobson, 1968, 2003), noted more than four decades ago when researchers found that teacher perceptions of student ability are self-fulfilling prophecies. In George Bernard Shaw's 1916 play *Pygmalion*, phonetics professor Henry Higgins transforms Cockney flower vendor Eliza Doolittle into an English lady with perfect diction. The Broadway musical *My Fair Lady* made the whole affair into lighthearted comedy. Shaw's more serious message was that perceptions become reality, for good or ill. As Eliza says in Act V,

> You see, really and truly, apart from the things anyone can pick up (the dressing and the proper way of speaking, and so on), the difference between a lady and a flower girl is not how she behaves, but how she's treated.

The education research discussed here suggests that the Eliza Doolittles of the study are not only our students, but also ourselves. When we expect that we have an impact on student achievement, we are right. When we expect that we are impotent, we are also right.

Skeptics may argue that the evidence in this study is not conclusive because the relationship between educators' attitudes and student achievement could have occurred *because* the schools were high-achieving in the first place. In other words, the leadership teams who believed that they made a positive difference could have simply been lucky enough to have high-achieving students, and those who believed that demographics were more influential could have begun with low-achieving students. It is easy enough to test this hypothesis by evaluating gain scores. Therefore, we returned to the original data set and compared the perceptions of leadership teams not with the student achievement scores, but with gains in student achievement. The results are even more striking when analyzing gains in achievement. In schools where leadership teams primarily attributed student achievement to student variables, the average gain between 2005 and 2006 scores on the 25 assessments was 6.14 percent. Yet in schools where leadership teams primarily attributed student achievement to faculty variables, the average gain was 18.4 percent. Whether starting with high- or low-achieving students, the team's perception acts as a self-fulfilling prophecy. When school leaders perceive that teachers are the predominant influence on student achievement, students and teachers alike rise to those expectations.

In sum, when teachers are given the opportunity to engage in action research on a sustained basis in a collaborative environment, three things happen:

• Teacher researchers frequently (although not always) have a direct and measurable impact on student achievement, behavior, and educational equity as a result of specific practices during their research.

• Whether or not the teachers' hypotheses are supported by their research, teacher researchers affect the professional practices of their colleagues.

• Participation in action research and the observation of and reflection on research results can lead to what Collins (2001) calls the *flywheel effect*. Effective professional practices are reinforced and repeated not only by the original teacher researchers but also by many other teachers who are influenced by these observations and practices.

From Research to the New Framework

This brings us to *Reframing Teacher Leadership to Improve Your School,* a contribution to the literature that is based on research rather than on speculation, personal preference, or philosophy. In my work around the world, I have yet to hear a teacher inquire about my uninformed opinion or idiosyncratic personal preference. Rather, teachers inquire about research, evidence, and experience. Therefore, this study is not the only one that offers insight to practitioners and policymakers. Rather, the greatest value from this initial research project is a framework in which teacher researchers will ask important questions, conduct investigations, discern inferences, and share their wisdom with colleagues.

In their seminal work *Wikinomics: How Mass Collaboration Changes Everything,* Don Tapscott and Anthony D. Williams (2006) invited readers to complete their text, transforming it from a stagnant document into a living work. Because an integral part of the new framework is the creation of a sustained network for professional excellence, the dialogue in this book will continue at the commercial-free Web site www.teacher-leadership.info. There readers can find a continuing series consisting of teacher research, commentary, questions, and insights from teacher researchers around the world. In addition, readers are invited to contribute their own findings, successes, challenges, disappointments, and triumphs. Therefore, even if you choose not to finish this book, your opportunity to participate is as close and fast as your nearest Internet connection.

Before you abandon the printed page for the Web, however, please allow me to make a case for the rest of the book. In the following pages, you will learn not only about cutting-edge research findings, but also about practical applications that can help improve student achievement and educational equity. You can learn how to have more influence as an educator and school leader. You can learn—not just from me, but from your colleagues—how to achieve more fun, greater satisfaction, and better results in every class.

2

THE LEADERSHIP IMPERATIVE

Educational leadership is more than a spot on a hierarchical organization chart. The quality and practice of leadership at every level have a demonstrable impact on organizational health in general and on student achievement in particular. Unfortunately, a leadership crisis looms, as almost half of school administrators will be eligible for retirement in the next half-decade and many contemporary leadership development efforts are ill suited for the task. Therefore, the gap between the reality and the potential for effective educational leadership will be bridged not by a repetition of prior administrative leadership practices, but rather by a new approach that embraces leadership at every level.

Leadership and Student Achievement

"We really can't expect leadership to influence student achievement," said the exasperated professor. "The connections are too indirect, particularly considering the impact of demographic characteristics." Stunned, I listened as the speaker droned on as a walking, talking example of learned helplessness. Unfortunately, he had picked precisely the right audience, leaders who wanted to hear that attempts to improve student achievement were goals beyond their abilities and that any expectations to the contrary were politically motivated attacks on the educational establishment. Worse yet, he had found plenty of documentary support in the pages of leading professional publications that, with an astonishing degree of conformity, published the same cover stories about the impotence of leaders, teachers, and schools to make a difference in student learning. It is hardly a news flash to suggest that poverty matters, that being hungry impairs learning, or that poor housing, nutrition, and health care are profoundly significant variables in the lives of students and families. Any sentient and socially conscious being can attest that demographic variables and student achievement have, in the arcane language of quantitative methodologists, covariance. Except, of course, when they don't.

Figure 2.1 (see p. 12) shows the relationship between student poverty, as represented by the percentage of students qualifying for free or reduced-price meals, and student achievement in 1998 in two districts that I have studied intensively: Norfolk Public Schools, Virginia; and the Metropolitan School District of Wayne Township (near the Indianapolis airport), Indiana. The "percentage proficient" refers to the results for reading on the Indiana Statewide Testing for Educational Progress for Indiana and the Standards of Learning Tests for Virginia. Essentially, the data indicate that educators need not bother with tests of academic achievement, because with a 75 percent degree of accuracy they can predict test performance based on the percentage of students in the free and reduced-price meals program in the school. In the words of one superintendent who was particularly provoked with me, "You show me the number of free or reduced-price lunch kids in a school, and I'll show you the test scores."

The declining line shows that as the percentage of students qualifying for free and reduced-price meals increased, the percentage of students scoring proficient or higher decreased. The R-squared coefficient suggests that about 75 percent of the variation in student performance was associated with student poverty.

It is a different story today, as Figure 2.2 (see p. 12) indicates. The relationship between poverty and student performance is essentially zero, and it is not possible to predict the performance of students and schools based on student poverty.

It is particularly noteworthy that these figures are based on *system-wide* data. The skeptics of high performance in high-poverty schools

Figure 2.1

The Typical Scenario:
Relationship Between Poverty and Student Achievement in 1998

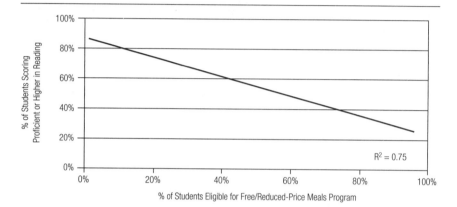

The data from Figure 2.1 and Figure 2.2 come from two urban school systems: Norfolk Public Schools, with a school population of more than 35,000 students, and the Metropolitan School District of Wayne Township in Indianapolis, Indiana, with a school population of more than 15,000 students. The scores on the vertical axis represent the percentage of students in each school who scored "proficient" or higher on state reading tests at the elementary, middle, and high school levels. The horizontal axis represents the percentages of students in each school who were eligible for free or reduced-price lunches. Figure 2.1 displays data from 1999, showing that the greater the percentage of students eligible for free/reduced-price lunch, the lower the achievement of students in reading. Figure 2.2 displays data for the same schools in 2007, showing that there is no relationship between free/reduced-price lunch eligibility and student proficiency.

Figure 2.2

Poverty and Student Achievement in 2007

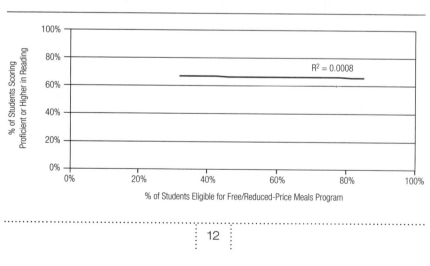

frequently cite the "Jaime Escalante Effect," referring to the calculus teacher in East Los Angeles who was featured in the film *Stand and Deliver*. Sure, the reasoning goes, an amazing teacher can achieve amazing results, but those results can't be replicated. Great teachers and great results in high-poverty environments are singularities, critics say, and their success stories serve only to discourage the hardworking teachers and administrators in high-poverty schools who are working as hard as they can but cannot make any progress. How much evidence is enough to sway the skeptics? Edmonds (1979) asked this question decades ago, before his untimely death. Yet every time there are suggestions that high-poverty students can do well (Carter, 1999; Haycock, 1999, 2001; Reeves, 2004b), critics complain that the examples are unique and not reproducible. Thus the question Edmonds raised still rings in the air: how much evidence is enough? A classroom is not enough, so we have school data. A single school is not enough, so we have system data. A single system is not enough, so we have multiple systems.

The relationship between leadership and student achievement is profound and *significant*, both in the statistical and in the practical sense of that term. Researchers have created a strong foundation for this relationship, including Goodlad (1984); Schmoker (1999, 2001, 2006); DuFour (DuFour, DuFour, Eaker, & Karhanek, 2004); Elmore (2000; Childress, Elmore, & Grossman, 2006); Marzano, Waters, and McNulty (2005); and the Wallace Foundation (Leithwood, Louis, Anderson, & Wahlstrom, 2004). Thus it is surprising to still hear the claim of leadership helplessness in the 21st century. Although research has grown from pebbles to mountains, the excuses remain surprisingly uncreative:

- The union won't let me change the format of meetings.
- My board won't let me change the schedule.
- Our staff isn't ready for changes in teaching strategies.
- The schedule can't be changed because of transportation.
- We tried change before, and it didn't work.
- Our culture is impervious to change.

However true these statements may be in some cases, the evidence of the relationship between leadership and student achievement is striking, even when other variables, including union contracts, board policies, time constraints, budget limits, and local culture are all held constant. Consider the following examples of specific leadership and teaching practices and student achievement. I initially explored the concept of Leadership Maps in 2006 in the ASCD publication *The Learning Leader* (Reeves, 2006a). In the months following publication, we gathered data on more than 129,000 students in more than 200 schools and noted the relationship between the degree of implementation of specific leadership and teaching strategies and student achievement. Just a few of the findings show the compelling relationship between leadership and learning.

When 10 percent or fewer of the teachers implemented writing and note taking as explicit teaching strategies in science classes, approximately 25 percent of the students scored proficient or higher on state examples. When 90 percent of teachers implemented the same activity, 79 percent of the students scored at the proficient level. It is important to note that teachers at the schools at the 10 percent level of implementation may have attended the same seminars, drunk the same coffee, and eaten the same bagels as their counterparts who instituted 90 percent implementation. The difference was not professional development; the difference was leadership and implementation. It is important to note that these are nonlinear relationships. In other words, although the difference between 90 percent implementation and 10 percent implementation is striking, one cannot infer that a 30 percent degree of implementation will yield three times better results than 10 percent implementation. In fact, for most of the teaching strategies we studied, there was not a significant positive impact on student achievement results until 90 percent of teachers participated in the strategies listed in Figure 2.3. This perhaps helps to explain one of the most vexing challenges in school improvement: taking good ideas and getting them to scale.

Figure 2.3 summarizes the data on student achievement and specific leadership strategies. Consider the typical scenario of new

Figure 2.3

How Depth of Implementation Affects Student Achievement

Classroom Strategy	Content Domain	Percent of Students Proficient with 10% Teacher Implementation	Percent of Students Proficient with 90% Teacher Implementation
Writing and note taking	Science	25%	79%
Aligning curriculum, assessment, instruction, and standards	Math	51%	81%
Displaying exemplary student work	Reading	52%	75%
Sharing big ideas and essential questions	English/ language arts	54%	82%
Monitoring performance in frequent and visible ways	Math	36%	71%
Including metaphors, similes, and analogies in daily practice	Science	50%	86%
Using questions, cues, and advance organizers	Science	25%	80%
Monitoring, measuring, and analyzing feedback to staff weekly	Science	25%	76%

professional development initiatives. Perhaps the principal attends a seminar. In the train-the-trainer fantasy, the principal is then to transfer this knowledge to the entire faculty. When that fails, the assistant principal, department heads, and grade-level chairs may also attend a seminar, read a book, or otherwise participate to one degree or another in the initiative. Although their enthusiasm may be genuine, the actual degree of implementation rarely breaks 10 percent of the entire faculty. When student achievement results remain stubbornly stagnant, the new initiative is declared a failure, and the principal sets out on another quest for the new, new thing. But as Figure 2.3 indicates, the problem was not in the initiative. The problem was in the degree of implementation. Thanks to Robert Marzano, Grant Wiggins, Mike Schmoker, Richard Elmore, and many other scholars and researchers, we know the powerful impact of specific teaching and leadership strategies on student achievement. Our quest for the new, new thing is doomed to futility. Far more meaningful, as the data suggest, will be the continuing quest for deeper implementation of the effective instructional and leadership initiatives we already have.

The list in Figure 2.3 is hardly exhaustive, but the point is clear. Deep implementation at the 90 percent level of teaching practice is associated with strikingly higher levels of student achievement. While writing these words, I can hear the chorus of "correlation is not causation." That is a true statement and an appropriate and necessary disclosure any time statistical associations are employed. But the "correlation is not causation" epithet has a rich history. For example, scientists at the American Tobacco Institute (Tobacco Documents Online, 1977) claimed that the association between cigarette smoking and lung cancer was only a correlation and did not prove a causal link. Indeed, they trotted out examples of people (like my paternal grandmother) who smoked like a chimney and lived to their 90s, and they conveniently ignored the legions of smokers who died prematurely.

Similarly, there are students who have been exposed to none of these teaching and leadership strategies who will perform well and students who have been exposed to all of these strategies who will fail. These exceptions test the rule, but do not disprove the rule. In fact, evidence of correlation can have profound importance, particularly when it occurs multiple times in a variety of contexts. I would never claim that any single strategy guarantees improved student achievement, yet the preponderance of the evidence is clear—leadership and teaching practices can influence student achievement. The essential question for the pages that follow is not "Do teaching and leadership matter?" but rather "How can we best expand and extend the most powerful teaching and leadership strategies?"

The Leadership Crisis

A radical transformation toward teacher leadership is not an option; it is a necessity. The nation, indeed the world, faces an acute shortage of leaders not only in education but also in every sector of society. Stephen Davis, Linda Darling-Hammond, Michelle LaPointe, and Debra Meyerson (2005) found that "a shortage of highly qualified principal candidates has been reported by school districts across the nation. In some parts of the country, nearly sixty percent of principals will retire, resign, or otherwise leave their positions within the next five years" (p. 4). The Thomas B. Fordham Institute and the Broad Foundation (2003) reported that "the United States is approaching a crisis in school leadership. Nearly 40 percent of its 92,000 principals will become eligible to retire in the next four years" (p. 39). That was five years ago, and the threat now looms larger.

The leadership crisis is not restricted to education. Nonprofit organizations, businesses, professional practices, hospitals, unions, and community organizations have all reported a pervasive shortage of leadership as a primary challenge for the 21st century. These shortfalls are more generally associated with a decline in social capital, as reported by Harvard professor Robert Putnam (2000).

Much of this crisis is a self-inflicted wound, created by decades in which youth leadership was studiously avoided by parents who preferred playdates coordinated by 18 sets of parents to the initiative of 18 kids who just wanted to play baseball. As a teacher, coach, volunteer, and parent, I have witnessed parents who objected to naming school newspaper editors, lest the students not selected as editors suffer hurt feelings, and who on similar grounds stifled team captains, class officers, club officers, leads in the school play, and a host of other student leadership opportunities. In fact, each of these student leadership roles is significantly related to future senior leadership roles in society (Reeves, 2007a). But our failure to provide opportunities for student leadership has left us with a generation of what pediatric neurologist Dr. Mel Levine calls "start-up adults" (2005) who are completely unprepared for adult responsibilities and leadership opportunities.

Leadership Development Is Broken

Peruse some of the world's leading educational, business, and government programs that are aimed at leaders in those fields. Whether those programs are offered by prestigious universities or executive education institutes, the high ratio of "leadership" to "management" courses is striking. The label "management" has fallen out of favor ever since the publication of the seminal article on the subject by Abraham Zalesnik (1977) in the *Harvard Business Review*. It is part of the common vocabulary of leadership students, if not practitioners, that leadership is lofty, visionary, insightful, and meaningful. Leaders, they intone, do the right thing, while their lesser management brethren merely do things right. However, those "hapless schleps" who are managers do the mundane work of creating a safe and secure school environment, providing meaningful teaching assignments, analyzing and applying student achievement data, and creating effective interventions for students in need. Those managers—characterized as nerdy and visionless by some—are actually the ones who catch great teachers doing things right and support them with the genuine appreciation and emotional intelligence that so-called visionary leaders only study at postgraduate seminars. Great leadership actually requires attention to the daily management tasks involved in running an organization.

Whenever I ask working school leaders about their greatest challenges, they consistently talk about three issues: people management, time management, and project management. They report with disappointment that their graduate programs in leadership, including those leading to a doctorate in the subject, were remarkably devoid of these essential subjects. The same is true on the national professional development circuit. Advertise an institute on cosmic leadership visions for the next 20 years and you can rent a Las Vegas ballroom; advertise an institute on the mundane tasks of management and you can occupy the dining area in the local Denny's restaurant just as soon as the Rotary Club vacates the space.

If you think that this analysis is too harsh, please consider your own leadership development experiences. In one school system after another, the trophy phenomenon is the norm. You'll hear the boast: "We had . . . [fill in the ellipses with your favorite national keynote speaker] here." However, once that keynote was over, the staff development department's next challenge was not deep implementation of anything, but rather booking the next unsightly mug shot to hang in the professional development trophy case. As this book went to press, I received a note from a superintendent who, with breathless enthusiasm, wanted to share a "new" speaker's presentation—precisely the same stale, fact-free, fawning, fatuous presentation I had heard more than 10 years earlier. This school leader enthused over "new" research that he simply did not have time to read, and in this case the new research was not actually research in the first place.

There are, fortunately, some wonderful exceptions to the rule. The University of California (UC) at San Diego, under the leadership of Dean Skip Meno and Educational Leadership Chair Kathleen Cohn, has created a remarkable example for other schools to follow. They begin with the assumption, rare in academia, that work in graduate school should be related to work in the real world. At UC San Diego, one can find four graduate students who all approach the same research question from different perspectives. They share literature reviews not because they are cheating but because they are colleagues. They challenge one another's methodologies not because they are sniping but because they seek to find the best methods to learn about leadership and learning. Similarly, the University of Oklahoma insists that students in its doctoral program in leadership conduct their research in an authentic environment directly related to their professional responsibilities. There are doubtless other shining examples of practicality and relevance.

However, in far too many universities, graduate study in leadership is abstract, without meaningful context, and unrelated to the daily challenges faced by educational leaders (Levine, 2005). Syllabi in these courses focus on national and global policy issues, as if graduates were to proceed from the classroom to the chair occupied by the secretary of education rather than to a school or district leadership post. This impractical orientation drives students away from studies directly relevant to their professional lives. Such an esoteric study of leadership is devoid of the passion and personal engagement that is at the very heart of real leadership in practice. It is precisely the same mistake that universities make when they require a student, working entirely alone, to conduct research on the importance of collaborative learning. The disconnection is carried into professional development when teachers are marched into a dark auditorium to learn, precisely in the same way with the same lecture, about the virtues of differentiated instruction.

Leadership Development Potential

The leadership shortage may be dire, but the leadership development potential is great, if only schools and systems will tap into the potential of teacher leadership. Even though 50,000 leaders will retire in the first few years that this book is in print, hundreds of thousands of teachers will be at the peak of their professional experience. Many of them are the quiet and unnoticed teacher leaders—the superhubs of networks of great performance (Reeves, 2006b). Even though they have not been asked to become administrative leaders, they nevertheless exercise leadership on a daily basis. These teacher leaders are not gossips but rather the people to whom everyone in the system—and many professionals outside the system—turn when they need a direct answer to a question about teaching practice. When teachers have a question about special education, assessment, instruction, or classroom management, they do not ask the principal or the central office; they ask a colleague. In Malcolm Gladwell's (2002) terms, teacher leaders are mavens, the people to whom everyone turns when they have a question. Almost every school and system has such a maven. The problem is that they are largely unknown to the hierarchy and almost certainly not a part of it.

In one example that galls me to this day, I found a maven in a 4th grade classroom. Gregg, a remarkable teacher, was the writing maven for the entire district. High school and middle school teachers routinely asked Gregg for advice on writing prompts and rubrics because Gregg was well known among his colleagues as the person who knew how to make writing achievement happen with students. It was hardly an accident that 100 percent of Gregg's students, including his second-language students, passed the state writing assessment. But when I reported to the district superintendent that Gregg was a remarkable teacher with exceptional influence on his colleagues throughout the district, the superintendent's response was perplexing. "I never thought he was one of our better teachers," the superintendent said. "He never comes to a meeting, never serves on a committee, never attends a boards meeting." It apparently never occurred to the superintendent that Gregg was too busy helping students and colleagues be successful. He did not have time for the political games involved in board meetings and committees. Gregg could be a great leader—a teacher leader—but in that environment he would be lucky to get tenure. Certainly he would not be identified as a future leader.

For every Gregg, quietly doing his job and influencing hundreds of colleagues, there is a self-aggrandizing egomaniac who leaps to every question, volunteers for every committee, and captures the attention of board members and senior leaders. The challenge of the New Framework for Teacher Leadership is to cast a wide net for the next generation of leaders, not only discovering those who call attention to themselves but also finding those many quiet teacher leaders who can serve our students and our society very well.

The Limits of Hierarchy

Harvard psychology professor Stanley Milgram (1967) is famous for many experiments, including the original "six degrees of separation"

study in which he demonstrated that people in two distant points—
Wichita, Kansas, and Cambridge, Massachusetts, for example—were
separated by a mean number of connections of 5.5, hence the genesis
of the phrase "six degrees of separation." A lesser-known but equally
important study conducted by Milgram was based on the children's
game called telephone, which involves one person whispering a story to
the next person, who in turn whispers the story to the third person in
the chain, and so on. Anyone who has played the game knows the
punch line—that by the fifth or sixth iteration of the story, the facts
have deteriorated and the story is meaningless. Milgram, however,
thought that Harvard graduate students would know better. How wrong
he was. He gave the students the details of a murder mystery, complete
with a killer, victim, and motive. But just like their 6-year-old counterparts, the graduate students flubbed the facts. By the fifth iteration of
the whispered story, these wise and cynical scholars conflated the victim with the perpetrator.

Every time a superintendent attends a seminar, then "whispers"
the findings to the deputy, who in turn whispers the findings to area
superintendents, who whisper to principals, who whisper to department
heads, who whisper to teachers . . . the point is made. Many times, professional development is no better than the children's game of telephone. Networks of teacher leaders, not hierarchical communication,
will be essential for the next school change initiative.

The Implementation Gap

Every organization—indeed, every person—suffers to some degree from a
gap between intention and action.[1] We know we should lose a few
pounds even as we reach for the extra piece of pizza. We know that we
should change the literacy schedule, even as we start the new school
year and leave the schedule unchanged. We know that engagement
among students and teachers is deteriorating, but we repeat the same
strategies for student and adult learning. When it comes to closing the

gap between the reality and the ideal performance—that is, closing the implementation gap—leadership makes the difference. The following section considers specific strategies that school leaders can employ to bring implementation closer to reality.

Create short-term wins. Psychologist Martha Beck (2006) marshals impressive evidence that individuals need immediate, continuing reinforcement to sustain meaningful changes. Tom Peters (2003) makes the same case for organizational change. Too many school initiatives provide their chief feedback through annual test score reports—results that are almost never delivered until it's too late to reinforce or modify teachers' or leaders' behavior. Effective leaders design plans in the spring and summer that will produce short-term wins within the first few weeks of school. For example, every two weeks, principals can post the percentage of the faculty that agreed on the score of a collaboratively evaluated student assignment. A higher percentage indicates a more effective collaboration and a clearer scoring guide. This type of effort is particularly important when turnover occurs during the summer and staff members are unintentionally sending very different signals to students about their expectations. Counselors can post behavioral data, signaling that as expectations are clearer and consistently communicated during the early days of the semester, the student climate improves. Faculty members can post visible evidence of interdisciplinary assignments and the resulting student work, showing colleagues and students a commitment to professional collaboration. Formative assessment (Ainsworth & Viegut, 2006; Chappuis, Stiggins, Arter, & Chappuis, 2004; Popham, 2006) is one important way to provide short-term wins throughout the year. It is absolutely vital that we understand the true meaning of formative assessment—an activity designed to give meaningful feedback to students and teachers and improve professional practices and student achievement. Tests designed only to render an evaluation cannot achieve the potential of assessment for learning that these assessment experts have suggested as an essential element of effective practice. In practice, formative assessment need not be lengthy or formal. Consider what happens in music classes every day. When students play a note incorrectly, the music teacher does not record the error in the grade book and inform the student's parents nine weeks later that the student needs to really work on the F-sharp. Music teachers continually assess student performance, stop when necessary to give specific feedback, and then immediately use that feedback to improve student performance. Lucy Calkins (1994) conducts writing classes for students of all ages with the same attention to formative assessment and immediate feedback.

The key to effective short-term wins is that the objectives are meaningful, are attainable, and provide immediate feedback to reinforce effective practice and modify ineffective practice. Without short-term wins, the pain of change often overwhelms the anticipated long-term benefits.

Recognize effective practices simply and clearly throughout the year. The Connecticut State Department of Education holds an annual "adult science fair"—an exposition in which professional practices and student achievement data are displayed on simple three-panel boards. Student data appear on one panel, adult actions are listed on the middle panel, and inferences and conclusions appear on the right-hand panel. Last year, more than 200 schools contributed displays. The Stupski Foundation in San Francisco uses a similar method to identify common leadership practices among effective grant recipients and to provide a clear and highly visible accountability mechanism that also serves as a professional learning opportunity. Schools throughout Connecticut, California, Nevada, Oklahoma, Georgia, and Indiana are involved in action research projects with a commitment to transparently sharing their results. They display not only achievement scores on formative assessments but also the professional practices associated with the scores. For example, an educator named Mitch Johnson found that during the first semester, his students who made the most extensive use of Cornell note taking earned scores on a national physics test that were twice as high as those who made the least use of this technique.

These displays are living documents, updated to provide a regular focal point for celebrating best practices.

Emphasize effectiveness, not popularity. Too many change efforts fail because leaders have underestimated the power of the prevailing culture in undermining change. To challenge that culture, leaders must be prepared to stand up for effective practice even if changes are initially unpopular. Teachers in every school know right now who is in danger of failure at the end of the year, and they know that with immediate intervention and extra time, many of those failures could be avoided. Yet one of the least popular actions any teacher or school leader can take is to change the schedule or curriculum of a student during the year. It is more convenient to wait for the failure at the end of the year and then attempt the same practices the following year, all the while hoping for different results. If the litmus test for goal achievement is the short-term popularity of the changes necessary to implement the goals, then the strategy is doomed. Change inevitably represents risk, loss, and fear, a triumvirate never associated with popularity.

Make the case for change compelling, and associate it with moral imperatives rather than compliance with external authority. An announcement that "we have to do this to comply with state and federal requirements" will never arouse the emotional engagement of the school staff. Instead of citing administrative requirements, inspire staff members with a call for their best: for example, "Student literacy is a civil right." "Faculty collaboration is the foundation of fairness." "Learning communities are the essence of respect."

The implementation gap will not be closed with another set of three-ring binders or announcements about the latest initiative. Close the gap with immediate wins, visible recognition of what works, a focus on effectiveness rather than popularity, and an appeal directly to the values that brought us all into this profession in the first place. The new framework provides a systematic way to take the lessons learned from teacher research and apply them in action. The next chapter introduces the elements of the framework and offers practical guidelines for placing it into action.

Note

1. Portions of this section previously appeared in "Closing the Implementation Gap" by Douglas B. Reeves, *Educational Leadership*, Vol. 64, No. 6, pp. 85–86. Adapted by permission of the Association for Supervision and Curriculum Development.

3

THE NEW FRAMEWORK
IN ACTION

Although the elements of the New Framework for Teacher Leadership are neither new nor surprising, the instances in which all of the elements are applied consistently and implemented with depth are, as the previous chapters have shown, exceptionally rare. It is essential to note, therefore, that it is not a new program, brand name, initiative, or other diversion that schools need. Rather, the critical imperative is for a new framework within which to implement and sustain effective leadership and teaching practices. The new framework contains seven elements that are part of a perpetual cycle, as shown in Figure 3.1. The framework does not lead to a destination, but rather illustrates a continuous process that begins with the recognition of a challenge and proceeds to research by teachers and leaders. The results of the research then can stimulate reflection and reinforcement. This stage is critical because many inquiry processes stall at this point. Will future actions of the system be based on the evidence, or will the filter for action research be a fact-free debate in which personal preferences, traditions, and opinions not only take precedence over evidence but also prevent a rational discussion of the evidence from taking place? The alternatives are stark, leading either to rejection of the subjective information and a return to the research drawing board or to resilience—the essence of learning organizations.

Recognition of Challenges

Barriers to change are notoriously difficult to overcome. Even when people recognize that there is a problem—perhaps a personal health crisis, a

Figure 3.1

The New Framework for Teacher Leadership

Note: The steps are labeled R_1 through R_7 to indicate stages in the process.

dramatic decline in student achievement, or deep personal and professional dissatisfaction—the distance from recognition to effective change is a vast chasm that few people and organizations cross. Imagine how much more difficult change efforts become, therefore, when even this fundamental first step of recognition is absent. "We're doing fine the way we are," one principal explained.[1] "Teachers are happy, students are happy, and parents are happy—I just don't see any reason to do things differently." Perhaps he had a point. Recognized by his peers as an award-winning administrator, he was widely popular with the staff. Indeed, they perceived the principal to be their protector, the one who would stand between their classrooms and intrusions from the central office. Parents also appeared to be content, as the school continued to enjoy support from a small group of active parents who volunteered, showered the teachers with praise, and expressed their appreciation to the principal.

Four consecutive years of declining student achievement were attributed, not so subtly, to changing demographics. Even though the evidence stood in striking contravention of the assertion, "I just don't see any reason to do things differently," the power of comfortable convention frequently exceeds the attraction of potential benefits to change. Moreover, the advocates of the status quo are frequently articulate and powerful—parents whose children are successful in school, college-educated professionals who are deeply vested in present practices, and competitive and winsome students who are well served by a system that allocates its bumper stickers to the chosen few on a regular basis. The missing voices in the conversation are the parents and students for whom current practices are not successful. The only way to break the deadlock is the first element of the framework—recognition.

In order for recognition of challenges to play a meaningful role in the framework, it must be transformed from an event into a process. When recognition is an event, it is characterized by information that is isolated, late, and disconnected from the daily reality of the school or system. Newspaper articles about district and school average scores, elaborate data analysis about the achievement of students based on scores in a previous year, and new initiatives, whether presented with breathless enthusiasm or stern commands, all are events. In response to these events, the reactions are predictable:

- "Sure, the district may be having some problems, but my class is just fine."
- "So last year's scores were down. Those kids have moved on, and it's too late for me to do anything about them."

- "You have a new initiative for me? I outlasted the past 10 of them, and I will outlast you. Just check out our professional development library for a litany of your predecessors, then put your ideas up on the shelf with the rest of them."

If a school or district has a process that makes sure relevant information reaches leaders and teachers in a timely, credible, and relevant manner, then effective recognition is possible. A case in point is Jenks Public Schools, winner of the 2005 Baldrige Award for school quality. The district stepped up its process of recognition in 2007 by creating proactive interventions in literacy and math for every high school student. High school faculty worked together to find the best predictors of academic trouble. Rather than wait for course failures, they found early warning indicators. For example, the combination of earning a D in a course and failing a criterion-referenced reading test was a strikingly accurate predictor of future failure. Equipped with this recognition, Jenks began giving students extra time in literacy and math. Teacher leadership was a critical part of the intervention program, with some of the district's most experienced and capable teachers assigned to work with the most challenging students. By intervening decisively and immediately—before a failure took place—the school achieved a dramatic reduction in 9th grade failures. The failure reduction was a comparison of the 2005–2006 school year with the 2006–2007 school year. Nevertheless, superintendent Kirby Lehman asserted, "We are not yet satisfied with the results" (Reeves, 2007b). This attitude echoes the pattern of successful systems such as the Metropolitan School District of Wayne Township (Magna Award winner) and Norfolk Public Schools (Broad Prize winner). Rather than rest on their laurels, they insisted on processes that continually recognized challenges. For districts like these, the process begins before the first day of school, when educators examine data on attendance, literacy, and teaching strategies and then make adjustments throughout the year. In Wayne Township, in particular, the reflection process has become deeply ingrained. Every school and central office department displays data not only about student performance but also about how well the professionals in the building or department are implementing effective practices. They never wait for the annual autopsy of state test scores for a moment of recognition. Rather, they engage in this essential first element of the framework every day of the year.

Research

Research holds an important, even hallowed, place in education. Perhaps it is too hallowed, as Ronald Wolk (2007), chairman of the board of Editorial Projects in Education, which publishes *Education Week*, recently noted:

> Research is not readily accessible—either physically or intellectually—to the potential users. . . . Even if research findings were widely available and written in clear prose that even a dimwit like me could understand, the reports would not be widely read. Most teachers are not consumers of research, nor are most principals or superintendents. (p. 38)

It is not, however, merely the availability and accessibility of research that is the issue. Too much research fails to meet teachers where they are, Wolk argues, leaving them in a sea of ambiguity:

> When one study claims small classes boost student achievement, another insists they do not. One study finds social promotion harmful; another says retention hurts children more. Money matters; no it does not. Vouchers work; no they do not. And on and on. This makes it easy for policy-makers and practitioners to get off the hook, because they can always find research results to rebut those they don't agree with. . . . By some perverted logic, we are told that we do not have enough research to justify trying something, but if we do not try it, how will we ever get any data to assess whether it works? (p. 38)

Quantitative studies. To be sure, large-scale quantitative experimental research, with random assignment of subjects to control and experimental groups, has a place in research. Major insights, such as the research of Charles Achilles (1999) on class size, result from this sort of long-term, well-designed, and carefully monitored research. Even where there is no random assignment to different treatments, a comparison of similar students in different leadership and teaching environments can yield useful insights, such as those suggested in the earlier chapters. The application of multivariate techniques allows researchers and evaluators to consider the extent to which leadership actions are related to student results while controlling for other factors, such as student demographic characteristics. That is precisely what University of Nevada, Las Vegas, researchers did in concluding that high-inquiry scores—leadership teams who attributed the causes of student achievement to teacher and leadership actions—were related to higher student achievement, even after controlling for demographic characteristics of students (Fernandez, 2006). Nevertheless, large-scale quantitative studies can set such a high threshold for research that policymakers and practitioners undervalue other research methodologies.

Evaluating research risks. The struggle for perfection in research can, as Wolk suggested, lead to paralysis. An even greater danger is that the quest for definitive answers leads either to the use of inappropriate and ethically questionable research practices, such as random assignment of students to unfavorable learning conditions (Reeves, 2002), or to the logical fallacy that the risk of change in the presence of potentially flawed evidence is greater than the risk of avoiding change. Consider the example of literacy interventions. Although there is substantial evidence that students who devote more time to a subject will demonstrate higher levels of proficiency (Brewster & Fager, 2000; Reeves, 2004a, 2006a), time is but one of many salient variables, including instructional quality, accurate feedback to students, motivation, and engagement. Nevertheless, time is an a priori condition for many other interventions. If a student is two or three grade levels behind in reading, then every strategy for instruction, feedback, motivation, and engagement will take time. Schools that embrace a variety of strategies but resolutely refuse to change the schedule and allocate more time are setting teachers and students up for failure. But, opponents to the schedule change will say, the research is inconclusive. We have examples of students who devoted extra time to literacy and who nevertheless failed. We have examples of teachers who, given extra time, simply had lower expectations and proceeded at a slower pace. Therefore, they conclude, unless the research gets more definitive, there is no reason to risk changing the schedule. This analysis of the risk of change is the critical fallacy in evaluating educational research.

Risk alternatives. Traditionally there are two sorts of errors that researchers can make. The first is the risk of confirming a hypothesis that is not true, and the second is the risk of failing to confirm a hypothesis that is true. These errors, sometimes labeled Type I and Type II and quantified with the terms *alpha* and *beta*, can seem somewhat obscure. But in fact, this analysis of the impact of alternative errors is at the very heart of educational research in general and of teacher research in particular. Let us avoid the jargon of research and speak plainly. Assume that I am evaluating some research that suggests that devoting extra time to literacy will be associated with improved results for my middle school students. The research is hardly perfect; there was no random assignment of students to different treatments, and the research itself appeared in a book rather than in a peer-reviewed scholarly journal. How shall we consider this research as we create the schedule for next year? One essential question is, what is the risk if I fail to give students extra literacy? There is substantial scholarly evidence that the longer we delay effective reading intervention, the more persistent the effects become. In fact, Elise Cappella and Rhona Weinstein (2001) reported that an 8th grade student who was not reading on grade level had an 85 percent chance of remaining below grade level throughout all of high school. Another essential question is, what is the risk if I give students extra literacy and they did not need it after all? The first risk that comes to mind is the "overly literate" 8th grader, a risk I will happily assume. Other risks—the sort that most frequently obliterate reform efforts—

include anger from middle school students and their parents who have been accustomed to making their own curriculum choices, anger from teachers whose class enrollments decline as low-achieving students are required to focus more on literacy and math, and anger from critics who lament that an emphasis on academics will ruin the arts and other elective classes. As this book goes to press, I can report that for the first time in years, Ben Davis High School in Indianapolis, Indiana, is hiring new elective teachers precisely because fewer students are repeating required literacy and math courses as a result of their mandatory intervention programs. In short, the fear that intervention would hurt elective courses was unfounded, and record numbers of students are enrolled in music and art. If the risk of change had been presumed to be greater than the risk of no change, then not only would the opportunities for elective teachers and students not have occurred, but thousands of additional course failures would also not have been prevented.

Qualitative research. Case studies and rich narrative descriptions can provide the story behind the numbers for educational research. Because qualitative research typically provides detailed observations about a limited number of subjects, the results cannot be generalized to a large population, a claim that few if any qualitative researchers make. Their aim is not to generalize, but to describe in a manner that is beyond the reach of quantitative research. The quantitative researcher can describe the strengths of variable interactions or student test performance, and the qualitative researcher can describe the cultural context of the school along with subtle behaviors of students and teachers that never appear next to a regression coefficient. The two methods need not be in competition but can complement one another in a meaningful way (Green, Camilli, & Elmore, 2006).

Action research. When teachers engage in action research, they are typically observing their own students and their own professional practices. From a research standpoint, such observations can be rife with difficulty, as the researcher is obviously biased—that is, teachers want their students to be successful and their teaching techniques to be effective. If this bias were overwhelming, one would never expect to hear action research reports that included frank acknowledgments that the results did not support the hypotheses. Yet in the study that was part of this book, teachers did report just such results.

In return for the risk of experimenter bias, the reward of local credibility and teachers' influence on one another is enormous. Moreover, from a methodological perspective, action research offers useful insights. It can be a perfect experiment in which all environmental variables are the same. The teacher, teacher qualifications, teacher background, content knowledge, classroom, students, budget, contract, parents, and curriculum all remain the same. The only change is a particular professional practice. Therefore, if that change is associated with a change in student results, it is quite possible that the professional practice is causally related to the change in student results.

Although an inference about causality should never be made based on a single action research project, it can open the door to the jury effect. Juries confronted with circumstantial evidence seldom recognize the proverbial smoking gun. Rather, they must piece together fact patterns such as systematic observations of quantitative researchers (perhaps a DNA expert); individual testimony of witnesses (the strange behavior of the defendant in the hours before the crime); and conflicting evidence from others (pernicious motives by the accuser, flaws in the research, or questions about the credibility of other witnesses). We trust the jury to make a high-stakes decision, however, based on the preponderance of evidence in a civil case or evidence beyond a reasonable doubt in a criminal case. Similarly, even though a single action research project may not be a definitive piece of evidence, it can be a crucial link in the chain that is the new framework.

After all, as Wolk (2007) reminds us, if research in its present form were sufficient to modify educational practice, we would already have done so. Action research by practicing teachers lends relevance and credibility to the body of educational research that is already present. Action researchers are not merely reporting the news but are saying to their colleagues, "This isn't some theoretical abstraction—this is *me*. I really did it with my students right here. It may not be perfect, but I know that it can work, so why not give it a try?" For educators who wish to conduct their own action research projects, the appendixes contain a model of a research proposal form (Appendix B), an evaluation rubric (Appendix C), a sample proposal (Appendix D), a sample report (Appendix E), a set of research review forms (Appendix F), and a sample participant report (Appendix G).

Results

For research to have meaning for teachers, results must be compelling, transparent, and public. In the study for this book, the action research teams engaged in three meetings throughout the year to compare notes and improve data-gathering protocols and analytical techniques. These culminated in a presentation similar in format to a science fair. The action research teams displayed three-panel boards that contained their student data, observations, results, and inferences. Each team also published a report that included the research question, hypothesis, sample characteristics, research methods, findings, conclusions, personal reflections, and suggestions for future research. Participants in the science fair included veteran educators who had participated in action research projects in the past but had not shared their findings in a public forum. This forum led directly to the next two elements of the framework: reflection and reinforcement.

Reflection

"Just get to the point," an impatient legislator might demand, "and tell us what works and what doesn't." It is a reasonable request, particularly from the perspective of a policymaker who had grown intolerant of jargon and equivocation from educational policy analysts. No matter what works in theory, the actual implementation of effective practice depends on providing teachers with the opportunity to reflect on research and consider the personal and professional implications of compelling research findings. In our study, teachers had opportunities for reflection during the action research process and at the end, when they shared their reflections publicly. Examples of reflections by teacher researchers include the following:

- I have really enjoyed undergoing this process, as it has made me more reflective as a practitioner because I have had to really consider the data, not just the results. I've also had to not only decide what skills to focus on, but also look for the best way to collect that information. Most of all, I really feel that my students have largely benefited, and that, after all, is the point.
- This action research project proves that there is an association between students using a formalized rubric and an improved understanding and articulation of their thoughts on a dance composition. When I refine and expand the way I approach teaching choreography next year, I will have a process from which to begin, with proven results attached to it.
- Parents are now more confident in the ways they interact with their children. Their activities at home have changed, and they put more emphasis on reading and writing. Their children have become more confident in their reading and writing and have been working harder studying and doing homework.
- We observed the pride and achievement of students as they rose from level to level on their basic math skills. The teachers also commented on the work ethics and the reduction in disciplinary referrals in their classes as a result of the focus and concentration the warm-up exercise had on their classes.

Not all the teacher reflections were positive, however. A mark of the integrity of the participants in this study is their forthright acknowledgment of frustration and challenge, such as the following:

- We found it very hard to implement teaming strategies with only two teachers, and attribute our lack of concrete results in academic performance to that. Furthermore, it was difficult to measure student gains due to the limitations of strategies and time.

- We should have involved more teachers in the project. Only four classes were included, and we did not discuss our project formally with other teachers. We could have created a survey regarding meta-cognitive strategies for the staff. This would have given us more data as to the amount of time teachers spend instructing metacognitive skills to students.

- I would organize my pre- and post- materials better. I would design a better survey to cover attitudes about school and life in general. I would explore the thinking of the accelerated students more. I would design a teacher-friendly form that students could take to their other teachers so I could find out if their attitude and grades have improved in other classes too. I would attempt to use a log.

Reflection is hardly a natural event among teaching professionals. It is not that they are unenthusiastic about reflection, but rather that few school schedules provide the time and structure for meaningful reflection on professional practices. Although many educators embrace the notion of professional learning communities, even the foremost proponents of the concept, Richard DuFour and colleagues (2004), lament the use of the label without the supporting structure, time, and leadership to allow for meaningful reflection.

Reinforcement

Why do most educational reform efforts fail? One important reason is the myth of linearity, reflected in Figure 3.2. In this myth, the leader notices a need for improvement in achievement, as reflected in the left-hand bar. One increment of effort is followed by one increment of results; a little more effort is then again reinforced by more results, and

Figure 3.2

The Myth of Linearity

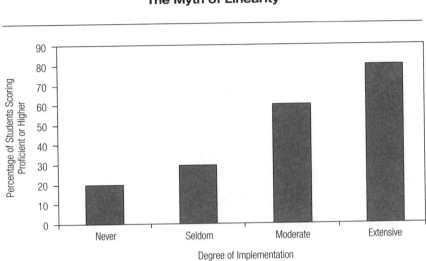

so forth. In such a mythical world of linear progress, teachers and policy-makers always receive reinforcement for their efforts, and this would sustain their efforts.

But in the world we inhabit, linearity is rarely, if ever, present. A far more common phenomenon is represented in Figure 3.3 (see p. 40), which displays the nonlinear impact of school improvement efforts. In the nonlinear model, the leader begins a new initiative implemented by a few true believers and enthusiasts, and then when evaluators and system leaders look at the results, they are astonished to see that *nothing happened.* The results are barely distinguishable from the results before implementation.

"More training for more administrators," suggests the helpful training vendor. Many dollars and hours later, the results are the same, with school and district average achievement barely budging. "Send the department chairs," suggests the training vendor. Amid growing skepticism, more dollars and hours are invested in more seminars, and the results remain anemic.

Figure 3.3

The Nonlinear Path of School Improvement

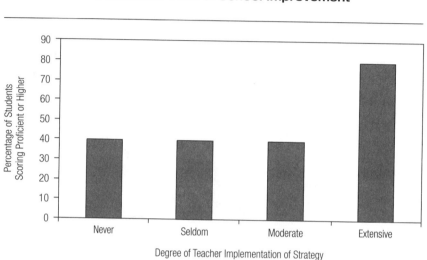

Perhaps, in a very rare case, someone will suggest that if the ultimate objective is deep implementation among 90 percent or more of the faculty, then an alternative approach, such as action research, followed by systematic analysis of results, public reflection, and meaningful reinforcement, would be a wise policy. However, well before deep teacher engagement happens, frustration sets in, the project is declared a failure, and the effort is abandoned. Besides, the leader who started that project has moved on, and now it is safe—in fact, it is expected—to criticize the previous project, find another initiative, and repeat the same cycle of limited implementation, no results, frustration, and abandonment.

Do these assumptions sound too theoretical? Consider real data from 15 schools in January 2007. (The data come from the Indiana Statewide Testing for Educational Progress for Metropolitan School District of Wayne Township; the tests were administered in the fall of 2006 and results were reported in January 2007.) As Figures 3.4, 3.5, and 3.6 (see p. 42) indicate, linearity is a myth. Only at deep levels of

Figure 3.4

Math Scores and Implementation of *Assessment for Learning*

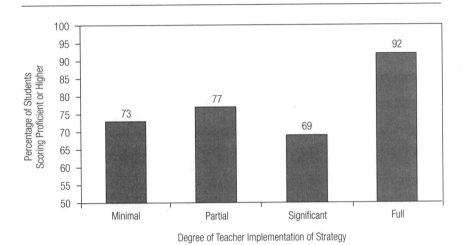

Degree of Teacher Implementation of Strategy

Figure 3.5

Language Arts Scores and Implementation of *Assessment for Learning*

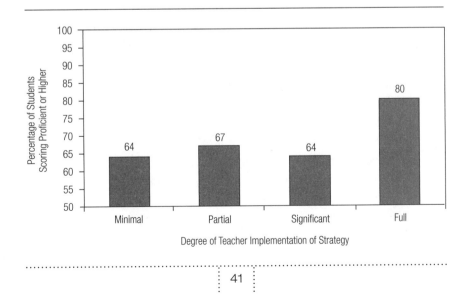

Degree of Teacher Implementation of Strategy

Figure 3.6

**Math Scores and Implementation
of *Five Easy Steps to a Balanced Math Program***

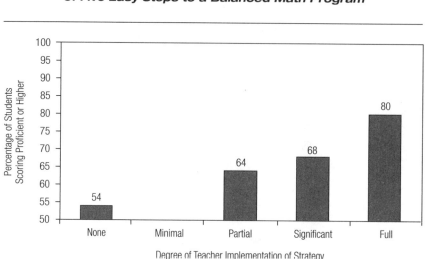

Degree of Teacher Implementation of Strategy

implementation did the efforts studied significantly improve student achievement. Note well that this is hardly an indictment of the instructional initiatives. Chappuis and colleagues (2004), noted for their advocacy of assessment for learning, and Ainsworth and Christinson (2007), creators of *Five Easy Steps to a Balanced Math Program*, are good friends whose work I deeply respect. Even though schools with low levels of implementation of similes, metaphors, note taking, summarization, and other strategies might claim to be "doing Marzano," the low levels of implementation and accompanying low results would undercut the claim. Similarly, some of the schools represented in the charts might claim to be "doing Stiggins" or "doing Ainsworth," but only those schools on the right-hand side of the charts crossed the divide from tepid claim to deep implementation.

Reinforcement, therefore, depends on consistent feedback about student achievement, professional practices, and leadership decision making. Annual test scores are demonstrably inadequate to serve to reinforce instructional strategies that require daily perseverance. In the words of one of the teacher researchers in this project, "This is the first time in 15 years of teaching I ever stuck with an initiative this long—16 weeks. Because I got results every week on the students and on my own practice, I was able to make midcourse corrections and stay with it. Before this, I would have given up long before the project was over."

The Fork in the Road

This chapter explored the first five elements of the new framework: recognition, research, results, reflection, and reinforcement. At this point, however, only the actions of teacher researchers and those over whom they exert direct influence have been considered. That is certainly significant, but it is not sufficient for sustained excellence throughout the entire system. If an educational enterprise is to take the knowledge gained from research and reflection and apply it throughout a learning organization, then the system must choose between two alternative criteria for decisions: evidence or the fact-free debate. These choices inexorably lead to the final elements of the system: resilience or rejection, subjects to be explored in the next chapter.

Note

1. All examples represent actual schools. In cases where the subjects have authorized the use of their names and locations, real names and school locations are used. Otherwise, as in this case, the facts are true, but the names and school identities are not used.

4

FROM REFLECTION TO RESILIENCE: CREATING THE NETWORK FOR A LEARNING ORGANIZATION

In the previous chapter we considered the first five elements of the new framework: recognition, research, results, reflection, and reinforcement. This chapter considers how different school systems react to the first five elements in strikingly different ways based on their decision-making culture. In an evidence-based culture, systems nurture and encourage teacher leaders and the insights they offer from their research. Even when the results are disappointing, the culture displaces blame with inquiry. The fundamental questions, then, are not "Who was wrong?" and "Where does the blame belong?" but rather "What can we learn from these results?" and "How can we save time and resources by applying these valuable lessons?" When the results are encouraging and validate effective teacher leadership practices, the response is not "How nice. Now please take your golden apple and don't call so much attention to yourself." Rather, the response to meaningful results from action research in learning organizations is one of celebration, encouragement, and genuine enthusiasm. Most important, the desired response to any research results—whether discouraging, encouraging, or perplexing—is resilience.

First, let us review the new framework in concept, and then take it from theory to application. Looking at Figure 4.1 and following the flow from R_1 to R_7, we have progressed to the decision criteria. If the fact-free debate prevails, we resort to an empty cycle of research that is temporarily reinforced, but ultimately goes nowhere. If the culture of evidence prevails, we can approach the ideal of resilience and the network necessary to support a learning organization. The path on the right-hand side

Figure 4.1

The New Framework—From Reinforcement to Resilience

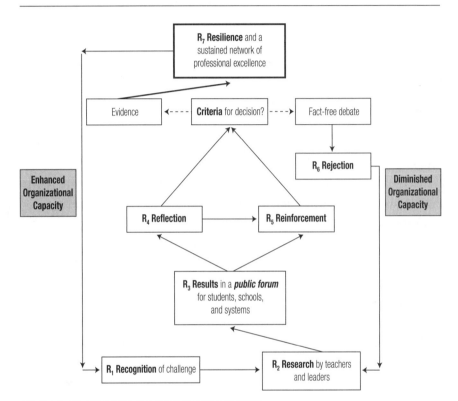

Note: The steps are labeled R_1 through R_7 to indicate stages in the process.

leads to diminished organizational capacity, but the path on the left-hand side leads to enhanced organizational capacity.

To be sure, the challenges are difficult as teacher leaders strive to achieve widespread implementation of action research. The goal will require a commitment of time for research, public sharing of results, and personal reflection. Data systems must be sufficiently sophisticated to provide frequent reinforcement and avoid the unproductive exercise in annual feedback that is too frequently late and irrelevant. However, even with adequate information systems, the framework remains incomplete.

During the last several years, data warehouses have proliferated in educational systems, and the commitment to decision-making processes based on data has never been higher. Nevertheless, the gap between what we know about teaching, leadership, and learning and what we're doing to transform that knowledge into action in schools remains surprisingly wide. The final element of the framework—resilience—suggests how leaders can gain personal and organizational momentum and survive the strains that undermine so many educational reforms.

Resilience in Perspective

When we think of the term *resilience* in common usage, the first image to spring to mind is a person who is optimistic, ebullient, and bouncing back from a few hard knocks, deftly recovering from adversity. Although this definition certainly is accurate, the *Concise Oxford Dictionary* (2001) comes through with nuances to language that we can easily forget. The first definition is, indeed, "the act of rebounding or springing back," just as our common usage suggests. The second definition, however, begins to unveil the deeper meaning of resilience, with particular implications for the context of teacher leadership. The *Oxford Dictionary*'s second definition of resilience is "revolt; recoil *from* something" (emphasis in original), such as resilience from oppression or dogma. There is also a technical scientific meaning of resilience, referring to the power of an object to resume its original shape after compression. In a phrase unlikely to find its way into the leadership literature, *Oxford* informs us that "the maximum value of the elastic strain energy in a unit volume that has not been permanently deformed is called the modulus of resilience." Yet it is precisely the "modulus of resilience" when applied to human, not mechanical, strain that determines the extent to which we can bounce back or, in *Oxford*'s harsh but precise language, be "permanently deformed."

To prevent yet another silly piece of jargon from entering the educational lexicon ("So *you're* the guy who spawned *modulus of resilience*—

thanks a *bunch*!"), let us consider an equally precise but more accessible adaptation of the scientific term associated with resilience: *the breaking point*. When teachers do exceptionally fine work that never becomes part of systemic improvement, they can accept it. After all, organizations are complex and intransigent entities, and every mature person accepts that some frustration is inevitable. Experienced professionals are, as *Oxford* suggests, able to deal with a certain degree of "elastic strain" as important insights into teaching and learning give way to the exigencies of the moment. But our endurance is not without limits. As frustration mounts upon frustration, as our devoted energy, research, diligence, and enthusiasm are pummeled by politics, intransigence, and indifference, we hit *the breaking point* professionally and emotionally. That is not jargon; that is reality. Our encounters with skepticism, cynicism, and rejection validate *Oxford*'s insight that an inherent part of resilience is recoiling from oppression and dogma. Let us consider the journey that teacher leaders must face as they move toward resilience.

Rejection

What's the first thing that comes into your mind when you read the word *rejection*? Perhaps, if you are a stunningly successful salesperson, you might say that each rejection is a step closer to a sale. If you are a forward in the National Basketball Association, a rejection might be something that you deliver, with a triumphant gesture to your opponent. But for most readers of this paragraph, rejection carries with it a far more melancholy emotional tone. Rejection to writers is an indication that they are not as talented as they thought they were. Rejection of aspiring college students is a threat to their hopes and dreams. Fear of rejection by a lover has spawned some of the most beautiful and heartbreaking poetry in the history of verse.

Why, then, should we be surprised that rejection for teachers is a visceral, emotional, and powerful experience? Teachers invest their intellect, creativity, energy, and emotion into an idea. With personal and professional courage, they engage in action research, exposing their successes and failures to the critical reviews of colleagues, friends, and strangers. Sometimes, although by no means always, their courage is rewarded with meaningful results—findings that save failures, save time, improve engagement, increase achievement, reduce discipline problems, and help move the agenda of every teacher and administrator in the school system. And then . . . *and then* . . . rejection. Sometimes the rejection is blunt: "Thank you for your idea, but that does not fit into our schedule at this time." More frequently, the rejection is silent. Projects, reports, posters, evidence, research, offers of help, all enter the black hole of indifference. The authors of indifference mean no harm. They have other priorities, after all. And the teachers, resilient creatures that they are, will try again and again. Ultimately, however, they will reach the breaking point and stop trying. The decline of teacher engagement—from enthusiasm to despair to disengagement—can be precipitous as well. The rest of this chapter addresses this crossroad.

Decision Criteria for Teacher Leadership

There is hardly a dearth of literature suggesting that, in concept at least, teacher leadership is a splendid idea. Consider the books on the subject that were published in a 24-month period:

- *Teacher Leadership That Strengthens Professional Practice* by Charlotte Danielson (2006)
- *Leadership Strategies for Teachers* by Eunice M. Merideth (2006)
- *Best Practices for Teacher Leadership: What Award-Winning Teachers Do for Their Professional Learning Communities* by Randi Stone and Prudence H. Cuper (2006)
- *Uncovering Teacher Leadership: Essays and Voices from the Field* by Richard H. Ackerman and Sarah V. Mackenzie (2007)
- *Connecting Teacher Leadership and School Improvement* by Joseph F. Murphy (2005)

- *Collaborative Teacher Leadership: How Teachers Can Foster Equitable Schools* by Martin L. Krovetz and Gilberto Arriaza (2006)
- *Lead with Me: A Principal's Guide to Teacher Leadership* by Gayle Moller and Anita Pankake (2006)
- *Leadership for Mortals: Developing and Sustaining Leaders of Learning* by Dean Fink (2005)
- *Teacher Leadership: Improving Teaching and Learning from Inside the Classroom* by Elaine L. Wilmore (2007)
- *Democratic Leadership in Education* by Phil Woods (2005)
- *Teachers Leading Change: Doing Research for School Improvement* by Judy Durrant and Gary Holden (2005)
- *From the Inside Out: How to Transform Your School to Increase Student Achievement: A Guide for Principals, Aspiring Principals, and Teacher Leaders* by Cheryl Samuel-Stover (2006)

Many of these volumes have some fine ideas and useful insights. I worry, however, about the gulf between concept and implementation when I consider the decision criteria employed in many schools. The alternatives before us are starkly different. Either decisions on leadership and teaching will be based on evidence, or they will be based on personal preference and tradition. The two are not necessarily mutually exclusive. There are sound research-based teaching strategies, such as explicit learning objectives, that have been used for decades. Others, such as Socratic dialogue, have endured over millennia not only because of the weight of tradition but also because of objective evidence of effectiveness.

Unfortunately, not every practice carries the weight of research that is proportionate to the weight of tradition. For example, despite decades of research (Guskey, 2002; Guskey & Bailey, 2001; Marzano, 2006; Reeves, 2004d) that grading as punishment is an ineffective and counterproductive strategy, the most common reason offered for the maintenance of toxic grading policies is not a new research breakthrough that contravenes decades of studies on the subject, but the mere assertion that "we don't have enough buy-in to make that change." Similarly, schedule changes that would allow students who are far behind in reading to catch up to their peers are dismissed without discussion because "our people won't accept that."

Fuhrman and Elmore (2004) and Schmoker (2006) have labeled this resistance "the buffer," a more benign term than is appropriate for such anti-intellectual conduct. Indifference to research, the elevation of tradition, personal preference over fact, and the embrace of the fact-free debate constitute the Maginot Line of education. In popular usage, *Maginot Line* connotes a poorly thought out and ultimately fruitless defensive strategy designed by a justly forgotten French general against an unstoppable German foe. The educational Maginot Line is actually worse than that. The similarities of the stakes between the fact-free debate and the folly of General Maginot's work are striking, with leaders' decisions resulting in the needless sacrifice of young lives.

Before readers conclude that this characterization is an exaggeration, a case overstated to make the point, they should consider educators' popular choices of pleasure reading. The best-selling *Teacher Man* (McCourt, 2005) and other works in the genre have a similar theme, the feckless administrator issuing irrational orders designed to ruin the lives of defenseless teachers. But part of our responsibility as teachers working to create a professional identity must be self-examination. I confess that I, too, bristle at administrative requirements and blanch at the suggestion that a dean, a principal, or an assistant principal can tell me what to do in either a university class or a middle school classroom, even though in the latter case I am a volunteer. But before I join the chorus of "this too shall pass" and vow to wait out the next administrative requirement, I must turn the lens inward and ask the question every true professional must ask: "Is my present practice as effective as I think it is?" As teachers, we must be willing to confront this question every day of our professional lives if teacher leadership is to become a reality rather than a slogan.

In the Wake of Rejection: Diminished Capacity

The new framework is not merely a prescription for a hopeful future, but a description of the very real present. As the right-hand side of Figure 4.1 indicates, even when the first few elements of the framework are in place, success is not guaranteed. Even when there is appropriate recognition of a challenge, research that is collaborative and effective, results displayed in a public forum, reinforcement of effective practice, and ample opportunities for reflection, the best practices in education can encounter a head-on collision with the fact-free debate.

Perhaps, as the new framework suggests, rejection will lead to another cycle of research. Perhaps we will continue to operate as "islands of excellence" (Reeves, 2006b) even as the sea around us remains unchanging. But as Admiral Hyman Rickover, father of the modern navy of immense ships, noted, the sea is so vast, and our boats are so small. Ultimately, the impact of the fact-free debate is Pyrrhic victory for the defenders of tradition and personal preference because the capacity for improvement of the entire system is diminished. Note that the future of public education is hardly assured. Every time I hear colleagues decline to engage in a research-based practice because it is insufficiently popular, I suggest that they get out their checkbooks and make donations to the voucher movement. In the past few years in particular, educational policy debates have become too easily polarized into an "us against them" debate. "Them" means the Attilas or, more au courant, the Darth Vaders and the Voldemorts, and "us" means the Luke Skywalkers and the Harry Potters. Let us abandon the fictional stereotypes and acknowledge that real policy debates demand complex details rather than easy demons. The price of admission to academic debate is the regular acknowledgment that one could be wrong, that one's hypotheses were in error, and that one's critics were right. I acknowledge that I have taken misguided tacks in my research, and have publicly admitted my embarrassing errors. What is even more embarrassing for our profession, however, is how few of the well-known experts, practicing teachers, and school administrators are willing to say, "I thought I had this idea right, but the evidence has proven otherwise." Every time we supplant evidence with presupposition, we support the fact-free debate. It seems like a small price to pay until we acknowledge the price paid by the entire system—a diminished capacity for organizational improvement.

If teacher leadership is to leap the gulf from appealing slogan to tough reality, we must first confront ourselves. Will action research become a time-consuming sop to feed our intellectual curiosity and collective ego, or will it become the serious basis for systemic reform? The choice depends not only on the administrators and policymakers whom we regularly critique, but also on our own decision criteria. In particular, I appeal to the veteran teachers who read these words. If you have been in our profession for 15, 20, or 30 years or more, then the most powerful words you can utter that will advance the cause of teacher leadership are, "I used to think this was true, but I've learned a few things over the decades and decided that I was wrong. The evidence suggests that my professional practice must now go in a new direction. . . ."

When professionals take this distinctly less popular path, then the door is at last opened to the penultimate stage of the new framework—resilience. Note well that I am not suggesting that teachers act like sheep and follow the latest fad proposed by traveling staff developers or well-intentioned administrators. Rather, I am asking that teachers choose a decision criterion based on the preponderance of the evidence rather than the predictability of popularity.

The Legacy of Resilience: Enhanced Capacity

When morale is low and, as Boyatzis and McKee (2005) suggest, dissonance is the default emotion, it is easy to forsake resilience for resentment. However, an educational system should commit to a transparent, consistent focus on improved student achievement based on systematic, continuous changes in teaching and leadership practice. Fortunately, when a system embraces that approach, the evidence is overwhelming that the dissonance default is abandoned. In 1998, only 11 percent of the elementary schools in Norfolk Public Schools in Virginia had more than half of the students achieving proficiency in reading. By 2005, the year in which the system won the Broad Prize in urban education, every single school had reached that benchmark. Not satisfied, however, teachers and administrators continued to challenge one another. Schools facing exceptional challenges are paired with schools that have overcome similar challenges. The two schools hold joint faculty meetings, host school visits, and share strategies as part of the culture of growth. Even as three different leaders have occupied the superintendent's chair, the school system has maintained the same accountability system and the same board goals for nine consecutive years. It is therefore no accident that two years after receiving national recognition from the Broad Foundation, systemic improvement continues at a remarkable pace. Here are just a few examples of data points from the 2007 results:

- 100 percent of high schools improved in end-of-course writing assessment.
  - 83 percent of elementary schools improved in English.
  - 82 percent of middle schools improved in English literature.
  - 100 percent of high schools improved in world history.
  - 100 percent of middle schools improved in math.
  - 100 percent of high schools improved in biology.
- In 11 schools, 100 percent of the students were proficient in at least one of the core academic subjects tested—writing, reading, science, social studies, or mathematics.
- The equity gap has closed to zero in some schools—a mathematical certainty when 100 percent of students achieve proficiency.
- More than 20 percent more minority students took and passed advanced placement examinations compared with the previous year.

A recitation of student achievement data does scant justice to the genuine enthusiasm, commitment, and resilience that permeate the entire system. Besides data displays of student academic work, a visitor would see evidence of professional practices in music, art, physical education, technology, and world languages. Next to the reports from schools are reports from every central office department. For example, a report demonstrates that accident and injury rates are down because of a systemic analysis of safety data and consequent improvements in professional practices. Delivery time from vendors, service from technology, support from curriculum departments, and a host of other documented improvements in professional practices are part of the stock-in-trade of a resilient system. It is not coincidental that when the district says "all means all"—the statement that has defined Norfolk's commitment to equity for a decade—the term is directed not only toward every student but also toward every adult. The best proof of sincerity is that the Board of Education posts data on its own performance. The board was aware, for example, that research evidence linked recognition of student academic success with improved achievement. Thus the board tracked its own record of recognizing students and teachers for academic success, posting quarterly graphs and demonstrating its improvement over two years. Accountability should not be merely something done to children or a threat to classroom teachers, but rather a systemwide ethic from the classroom to the boardroom. When such a pervasive focus occurs, there is a high probability that a resilient system will be sustained.

If the evidence is so compelling, then why is the new framework not already in place around the world? Why does the fact-free debate still hold sway when it is so manifestly toxic? Any consideration of systemic change must acknowledge the barriers to change, barriers that are astonishingly persistent and, in their own pernicious way, resilient. In the next chapter we consider those barriers and address specific strategies to overcome them.

5

BARRIERS TO TEACHER
LEADERSHIP

Imagine that you were attending a conference 20 years ago and a noted futurist was addressing the crowd of educators and administrators. With breathless enthusiasm and cocksure certainty, the onstage expert made one prediction after another of how the 21st century would be dramatically different. "Schools will be paperless," he claimed. "Students will not write anymore, but will simply dictate into the end of a pen, and then use voice recognition software to complete their assignments." Confident that technology, science, and engineering would transform every part of education, the speaker continued with his outlandish statements, full of hubris and confident that 20 years later no one would remember. But consider for a moment what would have been the most accurate predictions made 20 years ago about schools of today? Although no one would pay to hear it, and the accurate speech would have engendered a yawn or perhaps even shouts of disapproval, a remarkably prescient forecast from 20 years ago about the schools of today would have been the following:

> Twenty years from now in a very large number of schools, you really won't see much change. Desks in many schools will remain in rows while teachers lecture to students who are entirely disengaged. Grading policies will be about the same, as will schedules, credit hours, transcripts, and traditions such as final examinations. Even though we know now, and will know 20 years from now, that these are terrible practices, we'll keep doing them anyway. We'll continue to assign teachers to courses based on

personal preference and tradition rather than student needs. We'll continue to have the same amount of time for every student to complete the same task, even though we know that student learning needs and paces are different today and will be different 20 years from now. We have too many kids who are not reading on grade level today, and we'll have too many 20 years from now. We know the lifelong consequences of school failure today, and we'll be just about as indifferent to them 20 years from now. Legislators and school boards and superintendents can yell, threaten, test, and intimidate. They can do everything except change our professional practices. Sure, we'll have a lot more technology, but a lot of it will remain under the jurisdiction of the business and operations leadership of the district rather than instructional leadership—just the way it has been since the 1950s when the entire district had only one computer. We'll have a lot more computers 20 years from now, but the kids most likely to use them in pursuit of their education will be the same kids who have them today—that is, the economically advantaged kids who have computers at home anyway. Revolutionary change 20 years from now? Don't bet on it.

Such a statement would be dismissed by many in the audience as the words of a crank—just another veteran teacher who doesn't "get it," like the enlightened guru who promised extraordinary changes 20 years in the future. But any reasonable comparison of the crank to the guru on the basis of predictive accuracy would give the advantage to the skeptic that change could ever influence educational practices.

Why are the barriers to change so powerful? See if you recognize the following terms. They are associated with our reaction to a particular type of change:

- Denial
- Anger
- Bargaining
- Depression
- Acceptance

These are, of course, the stages of grief articulated by Dr. Elisabeth Kübler-Ross (1969). We can only confront the power of barriers to change when we recognize that, in fact, *change is death.* Change represents the death of past assumptions, practices, and comfort zones. The loss of those sources of security—my beliefs about students, teachers, and the entire enterprise of education—is threatening at a deeply personal level. Children can give up the illusions of Santa Claus and the Tooth Fairy far more easily than some of my colleagues will give up the illusions that punitive grading policies lead to improved student performance, that final exams and one-shot multiple-choice tests are effective and related to the world awaiting students after school, or that staff development based on lectures in dark auditoriums will ever transform professional practices.

When confronted with death, we engage in denial and anger, with acceptance only coming late, and to some not at all. Legend has it that Voltaire died cursing his confessor and that Beethoven expired shaking his fist. I hope to do the same, but I also hope that my reactions to changes short of death can be somewhat less antagonistic. If we hope to accept change, if not entirely welcome it, then we must consider the barriers to change and develop strategies to anticipate and overcome those barriers. Although many attribute resistance to change to aging teachers, set in their ways and impervious to change, my observations in thousands of schools suggest that we temper our stereotypes. I've witnessed teachers who have more than three decades of experience embrace new strategies, take on action research, and enthusiastically seek to make their 34th year in the profession better than their 33rd year. Conversely, some educators attain "ROAD" status, a military-inspired acronym for "retired on active duty," within minutes of securing tenure. Certainly able to change, but evidently unwilling to progress in their field, they have several miserable decades ahead of them. Fortunately, barriers to change can be identified and addressed in a forthright manner. This chapter considers the three Bs that are fundamental barriers to improved teacher leadership: blame, bureaucracy, and what we will euphemistically call "baloney."

Barrier #1: Blame

Efficacy is an exceptionally powerful psychological variable long associated with improved achievement by students and adults (Howard, 1995; Shaughnessy, 2004). When we feel efficacious, we feel that our actions make a difference. Efficacy is a sense of personal empowerment that gives us the confidence to take actions, engage in appropriate risks, and transmit our confidence to others, thus making our eventual success a self-fulfilling prophesy. Efficacy's evil twin is blame. When we blame our present or prospective failure on conditions we cannot influence—from the weather to the demographic circumstances of our students—then we forfeit efficacy and replace it with the status of a victim:

- "The kids are not speaking English at home—what do you expect me to do?"
- "When children are economically disadvantaged, they have fewer vocabulary words going into kindergarten than if they were wealthy. I can't change their first five years of life."
- "The cultural influences all around them undermine achievement. Even if I tried to recognize them for good work, they might get beat up on the way home."

Hardly a week passes when I do not hear some variation on these statements. Evidence from the 40-year-old Coleman report (Coleman, 1966) to more recent work seems to confirm our collective incapacity to influence student achievement. And when we believe those reports, the self-fulfilling prophecy continues. Astonishingly, the evidence presented in Chapter 1 suggests that not only teachers but also leaders who craft school plans attribute student achievement results to student characteristics rather than teaching and leadership.

How to confront blame as a barrier to teacher leadership? The new framework does not suggest easy prescriptions or commercial programs, but a process through which teachers are empowered to ask challenging questions and conduct research to test hypotheses and experiment with alternative strategies. When confronted with a blame statement about the intractable disadvantages of students not speaking English at home, the teacher leader will either search out or conduct action research to learn the conditions under which students who do not speak English at home can nevertheless succeed in schools. They will not discover the answer by looking at the typical litany of test scores based on district or school averages. Only when the classroom is the unit of analysis can we identify the promising practices of teachers who—as I have witnessed in action research projects in California, Connecticut, Virginia, and Indiana—are able to demonstrate that those students can perform at or above the levels of their English-only students. Their practices are hardly novel or mysterious. Many of them spend a great deal more time on English language literacy; three hours or more every day is not uncommon. Others use interesting techniques such as interactive journals in order to engage children who are not confident in their oral language skills. Others work with the music and art teachers to help build vivid associations between language and song and between vocabulary and vivid visual images. It is not just their techniques, however, that are so effective; it is their willingness to share their techniques in a public setting before their colleagues. When asked, "Why is Mr. Rawlins so effective with 3rd grade students who are learning English?" these teacher researchers will not settle for an ambiguous response such as, "Well, he's just an exceptional teacher." Even though Mr. Rawlins may indeed be exceptional, the professional practices that he uses with his students need not be exceptional. In fact, the new framework is the key to documenting and replicating those practices.

The blame barrier is at the heart of almost every level of resistance to change, implying that we are not really unwilling to change but that factors beyond our control make it impossible to change. When action research is prevalent, however, blame is punctured like an overinflated balloon. The claim of "I'd like to do it, but we just don't have the time" is punctured with the example of a teacher with the identical amount of available time who has invented a creative schedule that provides the time for literacy, collaboration, writing, or whatever was claimed to have been impossible for lack of time. The claim of "The union won't let me do it" is punctured by the teacher researcher operating under the same contract who demonstrates that he or she can honor a working agreement and also use alternative strategies when required. Indeed, union leaders in several states have enthusiastically endorsed teacher research and teacher leadership precisely because they demonstrate the exceptional flexibility that teachers have—if only we will stop assuming that they have none.

Of course, real barriers to change do exist, and sometimes those barriers include time, contracts, policies, and resources. However, the assertion that each of these areas renders teachers and administrators helpless—potted plants without a micron of efficacy—must be challenged. The helplessness hypothesis needs only a single example to prove its falsity.

Barrier #2: Bureaucracy

Schools are hierarchical organizations, with organizational charts and clear lines of authority—or so we have been told. But is hierarchy necessarily an accurate description of school influence patterns? In the context of considering change barriers, we can explore an alternative to hierarchy: the network. First, however, we must consider the limitations of hierarchy both as a necessary component of school culture and as an effective basis for organizational change.

Hierarchical change models fail because they are based on inaccurate assumptions about human beliefs and behavior. Despite an enormous investment in training, the creation of elaborate systems, and the issuance of endless streams of directives, leaders seem surprised when more training, systems, and directives rarely achieve the desired impact beyond the few islands of excellence. It is difficult to find evidentiary justification for the enthusiasm some writers (Bossidy & Charan, 2004) have for change initiatives when the record of their success is so dismal.

Uneven Enthusiasm

Sometimes the failure of change initiatives is explained by the much quoted 80/20 rule, where 80 percent of the performance is provided by 20 percent of the workers. "You always have the eager beavers," the leaders mutter, "and the rest of the organization will come along eventually." But the rest of the organization does not come along, and years after most change initiatives were started, disproportionate impact remains the rule. Studies of systems ranging from high-technology enterprises to people-intensive professional organizations suggest that the disproportionate impact of a few outstanding teams—the islands of excellence—can be extraordinary, but that most people outside these islands languish in mediocrity (Barabási, 2003). Figure 5.1 (see p. 62) illustrates a typical hierarchical organization. The boxes with names in them represent the islands of excellence—the 20 percent of the organization who embrace change and could, with the right organizational model, have exceptional influence. Within the hierarchical model, however, the islands of excellence languish in isolation. The change initiative leader at the top of Figure 5.1 announces a directive and expects her five subordinate leaders, one of whom is Harold, to carry out her instructions. Harold is the 20 percent who, in the mythology of the 80/20 rule, will disproportionately influence the other 80 percent of the organization. But he doesn't. In fact, he doesn't influence his own subordinates. The other islands of excellence in this organization—Steve, Andrea, Alex, and Julia—engage in what DuFour (DuFour et al., 2004) calls *private practice*. Therefore, even assuming that 20 percent of people embrace the leader's change, their isolation within the hierarchy limits their effect on organizational performance.

You have witnessed it dozens of times: the leader becomes enthusiastic about a change initiative, and senior management goes to an offsite retreat. New slogans, mission statements, and vision statements are generated, coffee cups and pens are emblazoned, extraordinary expenses in time and resources are consumed to extend the initiative throughout the organization, and . . . *nothing happens*. A few people embrace the

Figure 5.1

Hierarchical Change Model

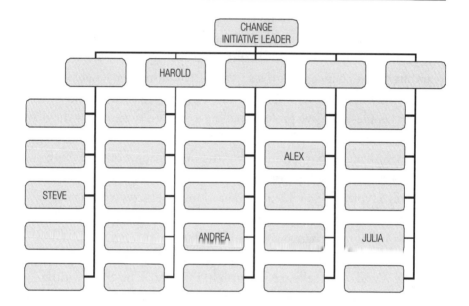

initiative, of course, but the leaders are reluctant to admit that those enthusiastic few had already been implementing the initiative without benefit of direction from headquarters.

The failure of hierarchical models is understandable when we consider how human belief systems are formed. Most leadership initiatives stem from a model that suggests that, as rational beings, humans will listen to the evidence, learn the new procedures, and follow directions. Maddeningly, however, the evidence is not enough, and new procedures, even when learned and applied in a training session, are not implemented. Why? Because behavioral change does not follow the creation of a belief system; it precedes it. Behavior does not stem from a rational consideration of evidence but from an emotional attachment to a trusted colleague. In 2004, the Gallup Organization[1] found that 55 percent of employees were not engaged with and 16 percent were actively disengaged from their organizations. Kouzes and Posner (2003a, 2003b) found high levels of distrust of leadership in their large-scale studies. One response to this state of affairs is for leaders to endeavor to become more credible, open, and trustworthy. But, as salutary as such leadership ambitions may be, employee disengagement is more likely a characteristic of organizations rather than merely a reflection of the leader. The Gallup Organization found that most employees in most organizations take their cues from a trusted colleague, not the boss, the employee manual, or a silver-tongued trainer (Rath & Clifton, 2004). In other words, even the best leaders cannot create the transformation from islands of excellence to systemic change by relying solely on a different boss, more employee manuals, or more eloquent trainers. The delusions of strategic plans and management charts notwithstanding, organizations are not hierarchies but networks.

The emerging science of networks suggests an alternative framework for systemic change. The traditional hierarchical model assumes that the intent of the leader can be distributed in a linear manner throughout an organization. In contrast, the network framework suggests that change throughout the system depends on a distinctly nonlinear communication through nodes, hubs, and superhubs. A *node* is any single point of contact in a network; a *hub* is a node with multiple connections to it. A *superhub* is that rare node in a network that connects to an exceptionally large number of other nodes and hubs. As noted, Figure 5.1 shows the traditional hierarchical network in which groups of nodes are connected to a hub superior to them. However, that is not the way networks, human or otherwise, work in reality. Figure 5.2 (see p. 64) is a close-up view of a simple network. In this model, the leadership change initiative is transmitted throughout the organization, but when people need advice, they do not ask the leader or the trainer. They ask Jill. Jill is the person Malcolm Gladwell (2002) calls a "maven," those relatively rare people who not only know a disproportionate number of other people but also seem to influence them. Jill is sought out for her advice on everything from restaurants to computers. Ask yourself and your

Figure 5.2

Close-Up View of Simple Network

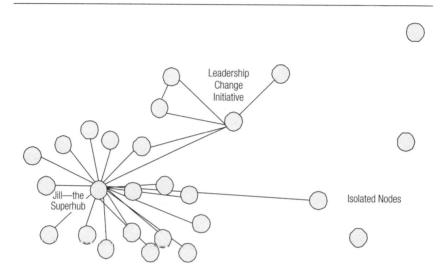

colleagues this question: if you needed help on a computer problem, whom would you ask for help? Based on surveys I conducted over 12 months with organizations large and small, the chances are less than 20 percent that you would ask tech support, the designated help desk, or the information technology department. Far more common responses include "my assistant," "my teenage daughter," or "Jill, the person down the hall who seems to know everything about computers." You can replicate this experiment in your own school. Ask, "If you needed help with a challenging student, whom would you ask?" The chances are slim that the first answer would be, "I'll ring up the assistant superintendent of instruction." In fact, the assistant superintendent of instruction is probably a wonderful person who is willing to help and delighted to be asked for his or her expertise. If hierarchy were really the solution, then challenges would go directly to the person in the hierarchy responsible for them. But we are creatures of networks, not hierarchies. Goleman (2006) concluded that humans are wired to be connected to one another, and we are more likely to connect to people we have casual contact with than to people separated by hierarchy and distance. Leaders who want to create effective and sustainable change initiatives can either continue to engage in the fantasy that their colleagues will conform to hierarchical expectations, or find their islands of excellence and leverage the enormous potential that they hold. They must, in brief, find Jill.

Finding Jill, however, is not easy. She may not appear on the organization chart—at least not in one of the hierarchical boxes—and may appear to be unexceptional. Consider again the case of Gregg, the 4th grade teacher I interviewed in Colorado. Gregg was not seeking positional authority associated with membership on a committee or the pursuit of an administrative title. He wielded far more influence in his position as a superhub in the district's network. How powerful can one superhub be? In education, Benjamin Bloom has influenced an extraordinary number of today's leading writers, researchers, and teachers, which is a result not only of his long tenure at the University of Chicago, but also of his many graduate students and colleagues who went on to have long and prolific careers. Guskey (2005) identified an exceptional number of deans, professors, and senior educational policymakers who have been influenced by the teaching of this one remarkable educator. We know with benefit of hindsight how profound Bloom's influence was on the field, but few would have guessed this at the nascent stage of his career. Similarly, the magnitude of Gregg's influence extends to literally thousands of students, many of whom he will never know. Certainly people in the hierarchy above him appeared not to know of his influence. Yet Gregg's quiet professional practices are more likely to influence his colleagues than any of the speakers, initiatives, and programs to which they will be exposed.

Finding the Network Superhubs

Networks with nodes, hubs, and superhubs are pervasive, as Albert-Laszlo Barabási (2003) impressively documented, in biology, across the Internet, and—most important for this discussion—in organizations. We may not be able to create Jill, but we can find Jill and then nurture, appreciate, and leverage Jill's superhub status so that information is dispersed, rumors are squelched, skills are shared, and values are modeled. "Networks do not offer a miracle drug, a strategy that makes you invincible in any business environment," Barabási warned. "The truly important role networks play is in helping existing organizations adapt to rapidly changing market conditions" (2003, p. 216).

To find the superhubs, we must learn not only their characteristics but also the characteristics of the network within which they reside. Barabási (2003) suggested that the network is a web without a spider. He explained, "In the absence of a spider, there is no meticulous design behind these networks either. Real networks are self-organized. They offer a vivid example of how the independent actions of millions of nodes and links lead to spectacular emergent behavior" (p. 221). Therefore, we must acknowledge something that leaders of organizational change are reluctant to admit: Jill is a volunteer, not a conscript. To find Jill, we must first create a network map. Jill is the colleague most people ask for advice when they have a work-related problem, if they ask at all. Some people stubbornly refuse to ask for help, and a few follow the chain of command. The potential power of Jill in practice is extraordinary, particularly compared with the single lines of a hierarchical network in Figure 5.1 or the overwhelming odds against a single superhub in a random network.

In one organization we observed, we found Jill simply by asking people which colleague they would ask for advice. Also important is the discovery of where Jill is not. Jill, it turned out, was not in the executive suite or in the professional development department. In fact, it was a stroke of great luck that Jill was an employee in the same school system. Some of the people most influential in organizational change initiatives may not even be members of the organization, nor do they necessarily have job titles associated with administrative authority. When people identify change mavens, close on Jill's heels are largely unseen networks of spouses, children, parents, friends, and casual acquaintances. Your employees' mothers-in-law, golfing buddies, and neighbors have a greater impact on how your employees view organizational change than do many administrators and senior executives. On some occasions, Jill may desire to join the ranks of organizational leadership, in which case this treasure of influence, this superhub, should receive development, promotion, and leadership opportunities. But for the most part, leaders must accept Jill on her terms. We can observe her work, listen to her advice, and emulate some of her communication patterns. But we cannot mandate that Jill become anything other than who she is: an extraordinary source of power and influence within the organization. Jill does not need, nor will she necessarily listen to, our exhortations and commands. It's the other way around—leaders need to listen to Jill, for what they hear from this superhub will be a taste of what the entire organization is hearing.

Some readers may regard any alternative to hierarchy as a pipe dream. "Networks would be nice," they reason, "but that's just not the real world." My gentle reply would be the following: if Isaac Newton were addressing educational leaders on the subject of gravity, he would not ask for a vote about who believed in gravity, nor would he consider whether there was sufficient organizational buy-in for the concept of gravity. He would throw an apple at the reluctant observers and say, "That's gravity!" So it is with networks. My purpose is not to persuade the reader that networks exist, because that would be as silly as persuading them that gravity exists. The central challenge of leadership is the understanding, identification, and deployment of networks for positive results. Leaders should abandon the concept that they can contrive networks through organizational charts or change initiatives. Rather, they must recognize the networks that they already have, recognize their hubs and superhubs, and—this is the greatest leadership technique of all—listen.

Barrier #3: Baloney

Even if we are able to break down the barriers created by blame and bureaucracy, a third obstacle to teacher leadership remains: a barrier we will politely label "baloney." *Merriam-Webster Online Dictionary* (2007) offers the following definition: "pretentious nonsense." In the context of the barriers to teacher leadership, baloney is the unappetizing combination of ingredients including superstition, prejudice, and deeply held convictions, all unburdened by evidence. The culture of baloney is the polar opposite of the culture of evidence, because it undermines research and teacher leadership even before they start. I recently spoke to a group of educators and administrators who expressed deep divisions about a prospective change in school policy. "I understand that there are disagreements on this matter, and I respect the different points of view," I said. "Can we at least agree, however, that the way we will resolve this question will be not on the strength of our opinions, but on the evidence that we find? Could we at least agree to gather data, determine which alternative is best supported by the data, and then let the evidence guide our final decision? I realize that some people will continue to disagree with the decision, but is it possible that we can agree on the process?" Stony silence followed. The culture apparently was based on administrators imposing policies based on their authority rather than evidence. With Newtonian precision, an equal and opposite reaction came from teachers, who had a culture of opposing those same policies based on their authority within the classroom rather than evidence. Neither side was willing to submit its case to an evidentiary determination.

Promising research, however, suggests that this stalemate may be the exception rather than the rule. Kim and Mauborgne (2004) reported the fascinating finding that people were far more likely to support a change in policy when they believed that the process of decision making was fair, even when they disagreed with the decision. In fact, their satisfaction was higher when an unpopular decision was preceded by a good decision process than when employees liked the final decision but found the decision process unfair, noninclusive, and irrational. In other words, embracing a culture of evidence and rejecting a culture of baloney will not always create popular decisions, but it will create more overall satisfaction, even when decisions are not popular.

Teacher leadership offers exceptional promise for student achievement and faculty morale. Overcoming the barriers of blame, bureaucracy, and baloney is challenging, but the results are compelling. When we replace blame with efficacy, supplant bureaucracy with networks, and give evidence power over baloney, we open the doors for the new framework. In the final chapter, we explore how schools, systems, and governing bodies can enhance and support teacher leadership.

Note

1. According to an interview with Barb Sanford, managing editor of the *Gallup Management Journal*, on August 11, 2005, results of this survey are based on nationally representative samples of about 1,000 employed adults age 18 and older. Interviews were conducted by telephone from October 2000 to October 2004 by the Gallup Organization. For results based on samples of this size, one can say with 95 percent confidence that the error attributable to sampling and other random effects could be plus or minus 3 percentage points. For findings based on subgroups, the sampling error would be greater.

6

HOW SYSTEMS SUPPORT THE NEW FRAMEWORK FOR TEACHER LEADERSHIP

This book has made the case that teacher leadership is a systems issue. It is neither a slogan nor a fad, but a fact. The single greatest influence on the professional practices of teachers is the direct observation of other teachers. With systemic support, that network of direct observation can transform a large and complex system with dramatic effect. But what if, as with so many educational reforms, teacher leadership is honored with no more than a label, a brief passing reference from senior leadership before they proceed on to the next new thing?

Perhaps teacher leadership can survive in the short term without systemic support. After all, great teachers have always identified challenges, engaged in research, shared their results, and influenced practice. Without systemic support, however, great teachers remain islands of excellence, surrounded by oceans of well-intentioned teachers who lack the information, skills, and opportunities for practice that distinguish their most effective colleagues. The new framework describes two stark alternatives: rejection or resilience. When teacher initiative and insight are repeatedly followed by rejection, the lack of systemic support will undermine the framework and render teacher leadership nothing more than a hollow slogan. When policymakers, administrators, and leaders at every level embrace the framework, then they contribute to the establishment of a resilient system that will endure disappointments and hardships because of the confidence in a culture of evidence and support for teacher leadership. In this chapter, we consider system support at the school, district, and state and provincial levels and offer suggestions for how national governments can enhance and support teacher leadership.

How School Administrators Support Teacher Leadership

Embracing teacher leadership does not diminish the role of the principal and other administrators. In fact, they have an enormously important additional responsibility: that of talent scout, constantly on the prowl for effective practice. Rather than policing compliance and meticulously identifying what teachers do wrong, administrators who support teacher leadership relentlessly "catch teachers doing something right" and view that as an essential part of their daily activities.

A few years ago, the Franklin T. Simpson-Waverly Elementary School in Hartford, Connecticut, was an unlikely candidate to become an island of excellence. With 94 percent of students eligible for free or reduced-price meals and many children living with grandparents, academic achievement was suffering, and social, emotional, and school challenges were enormous. Mobility was high, and morale and motivation were low. The school leader, James Thompson, might have been expected to implement a strict top-down management approach, treating his faculty as robots and expecting them to carry out instructions without making an intellectual contribution to the enterprise. Instead, Dr. Thompson called himself the chief talent scout and made it his business to discover, document, and replicate excellent teaching practices within the school.

Dr. Thompson relentlessly identified his in-house experts, finding and nurturing the Jills within the school. In order to make the sharing of both effective practices and mistakes a risk-free endeavor, the principal was emphatic that the focus of this process was not evaluation, but learning. "When making decisions," said Dr. Thompson, "you should not be in isolation. To know how you are doing, for validation and improvement, you need your peers" (Reeves, 2006b).

In fact, there had always been examples of excellent practice at Franklin T. Simpson-Waverly, but they were isolated, with private practitioners engaged in private practice. By introducing systematic networking, the islands were no longer isolated, and their influence extended throughout the school. As a result, Simpson-Waverly now outperforms some of its more affluent suburban neighbors on measures of academic achievement, and the school has become a statewide model for academic excellence, a true superhub of educational impact. In addition, faculty and administrators from other schools within the district, from the central office, and from other districts frequently visit the school to observe their collaborative meetings.

The Science Fair

Another technique to promote teacher leadership and transform islands of excellence into systemic change is the adult science fair, mentioned in Chapter 2. A growing number of schools throughout the United States use this approach. The most common model is a simple three-panel display board, with student achievement results on the left-hand panel, teacher and leadership actions on the middle panel, and the conclusions and inferences from the data on the right-hand panel. Appendix H contains simple instructions for how the science fair concept can be used. Appendix I includes instructions for the treasure hunt that helps participants make maximum use of the professional learning from the science fair.

Teachers in Wayne Township Metropolitan School District in Indianapolis, Indiana, make the science fair part of their regular summer leadership retreat. Principals have dug deep into practices such as how bus drivers contributed to improved safety and order, successes in literacy programs, and reductions in secondary school truancy and tardiness. In Gilroy, California, the science fair revealed individual classrooms where the performance of second-language students exceeded that of English-only students, and thus the district was able to identify and replicate excellent teacher practices. In Cobb County, Georgia, the same technique was used to identify practices associated with dramatic increases in advanced placement success. In Norfolk, Virginia, the science fair allowed district leaders to identify classroom teachers who had exceptional success working with special education students. This intense focus on classroom-by-classroom analysis of actual teaching practice reveals techniques that are never apparent from the typical accountability report that is only a list of test scores. Moreover, most reports contain only school averages, when the most revealing data—the path to finding Jill—lie in classroom data and analysis of classroom practices.

Practical Ways to Promote Networks in Schools

The following ideas can help teachers get started sharing effective strategies among peers.

- Ask teachers to keep weekly journals on just two students, one of whom is underperforming and one of whom needs to be challenged beyond the current curriculum. Have them consider questions such as, What did you try? What worked? What didn't? What's next? Taken alone, we can be reluctant to draw many conclusions from such isolated observations. But when the entire faculty contributes to such an effort, isolated practices can be highlighted and shared frequently and systematically.
- Make faculty meetings an announcement-free zone, in which all administrative announcements are relegated to paper or e-mail, and all faculty meeting time is focused on professional sharing.
- Create a best-practices book every year, with each teacher contributing just a single page. Present the booklet as a going-away present at the end of each year, and as a welcome gift for new teachers at the beginning of each year. It seems like a small effort at first, but over the course of time, the request for just a single page leads to a book-length compendium that recognizes great local practice. Moreover, you will see evidence that the great work of a single teacher will influence the best practices of colleagues years into the future.
- Create a best-practices club with student involvement. *Education Week* (Rothstein, 2006) commented that Lexington High School created a best-practices club in which students helped identify teaching

practices that positively affected learning. Teachers were enthusiastic, and students saw themselves as part of the learning enterprise.

- Allow anonymous sharing of best practices, designating time during each faculty meeting and professional development session for sharing questions, challenges, and success stories. In some schools, the cultural environment may regard the sharing of success stories as showing off or provoking inappropriate comparisons among teachers. Don't wait for the culture to change; create opportunities for teachers to submit success stories anonymously and then publicize them. Teachers know who the most effective professionals are, but the technique of anonymity shields the authors of success stories from accusations of self-promotion.

Principals who encourage teacher leadership understand that genuine leadership has less to do with title and position than it does with influence. These principals maximize leadership effectiveness by having every single teacher take responsibility for documenting and sharing examples of effective professional practices.

District and System Support for Teacher Leadership

The history of district support for teacher leadership is checkered, with the term *TOSA*, or "teacher on special assignment," used as a code for a simple cost-saving strategy: get teachers to do the work formerly done by central office administrators, but pay teacher salaries rather than the higher pay of administrators. In this context, the phrase "teacher leadership" takes a cynical turn and fuels long-held distrust between classroom teachers and the central office. Artificial teacher leadership is not limited to the TOSA designation. In many school districts, labels such as "academic coach" or "instructional mentor" or even the apparently managerial title of "director" have been applied to teachers who occupy positions in schools and central office buildings, but who have neither administrative authority nor much in the way of direct contact with students. Some instructional coaches spend 90 to 100 percent of their time in classrooms with students and teachers, genuinely earning the title "coach" as someone who is providing direct assistance to improve classroom instruction. Others with the identical title remain isolated in separate rooms, writing curriculum documents and lesson plans, attending staff development workshops and analyzing data, but remaining assiduously out of direct contact with classroom teachers and students. Fortunately, there are specific steps that superintendents and district leaders can take to support teacher leadership.

First, establish the classroom as the central unit of analysis in all district-generated data, professional development plans, and teacher leadership initiatives. The least helpful data point in education right now is the district average, followed closely by the school average. I understand that many state accountability systems focus on the district and the school as units of analysis, but that approach is about as helpful as reporting the average temperature or average weight of a community, neighborhood, or family. The focus on the average will never allow policymakers, leaders, and practitioners to understand their most and least effective practices. Although the district and school average may yield a profound gap between economically advantaged and disadvantaged children, we will never gain insight into how to address that inequity if we do not identify individual classrooms in which economically disadvantaged children are doing well. Similarly, there are individual classrooms where English language learners perform at or above their English-only counterparts, where minority students perform as well as nonminority students, and where special education students meet state standards. These classrooms, however, remain in the realm of "invisible excellence" in districts whose data systems reveal only system and building averages. Almost a decade into the 21st century, where multimillion-dollar data warehouses have consumed enormous amounts of available educational resources, it remains common practice for principals and teachers to use index cards, chart paper, pens, and markers for tracking student progress to obtain meaningful data at the classroom level. I have heard many claims of sophisticated data manipulation and witnessed wide-eyed enthusiasm over the slice-and-dice capabilities of one database after another. Yet administrators and teachers who want information about *their students* in a comprehensive and focused format continue to do it themselves with tools that are more than a century old, when the new technology was a Big Chief tablet and the No. 2 pencil. District leaders, therefore, have a responsibility to demand more in return for the investment they are making in technology. They can start by placing all instructional technology departments under the domain of the instructional leadership of the district. When databases are constructed from the perspective of the business office, we should not be surprised that the obvious boxes in the hierarchy—district and schools—are the unit of analysis. When databases are constructed from the perspective of instructional leadership, we would expect that students and classrooms are the focus of analysis, and the architecture of data systems will follow based on a decidedly different premise.

The obligation of the central office to focus on classrooms extends well beyond the design of data systems. Well-intentioned initiatives in professional development and teacher leadership remain mired in outmoded concepts of training that are redolent of the Taylorist movement in which the uniform motion of factory workers was the hallmark of a successful enterprise. I recently received another enthusiastic claim by a district leader that the schools were engaged in a "trainer of trainers" program. This leader apparently was not considering that, from a classroom perspective, the teacher must necessarily be a "trainee of trainees." This is the polar opposite of genuine teacher leadership. This approach screams that influence, information, and insight all stem from administrators imbued with mystical authority and that classroom teachers are passive vessels, waiting to be filled. Once we make the classroom the unit of analysis, professional development is radically transformed. When system leaders wish to have an initiative with widespread and deep implementation, the hierarchical model is rejected along with Taylorist principles of uniformity. These approaches are replaced with action research, science fairs, and peer mentorship, which are direct reflections of the new framework. Central office leaders take the risk that the network may be less consistent than the hierarchy while recognizing that the hierarchy itself was consistent only in an illusory manner. That is, the three-ring binders in the central office were consistent, but the delivery and implementation at the classroom level were wildly inconsistent. Taylorist uniformity screams disrespect: "You've been here for 28 years, and you've been doing it wrong, so listen to someone who hasn't been around a classroom for 30 years and you can learn how to do it right." By contrast, the new framework screams respect, honoring teachers not merely for being veterans or for having advanced degrees or for being bellicose—but for being effective. Superintendents must take the impact of respect for employees seriously, as it is directly related to one of the key challenges of educational leadership today—retaining and recruiting teachers and leaders. Although salary and benefits are important, Aretha Franklin's focus on R-E-S-P-E-C-T has a substantial research foundation. David Sirota, Louis Mischkind, and Michael Meltzer (as cited in *Training Today: R-E-S-P-E-C-T*, 2006) surveyed more than 370,000 employees with astonishing results. They found that 63 percent of respondents who did not believe their employers treated them with respect intended to leave their positions within a two-year time frame. In comparison, only 19 percent of those who felt their employers treated them like adults intended to leave within two years. Further, employees who reported that they felt "very good" about their at-work treatment were more than three times as enthusiastic as respondents who felt just "good" about how they were treated.

When more than a quarter-million employees tell us something, perhaps system-level leaders should listen. If we are persuaded that respect is important, then how can we best demonstrate it? Let the data speak. The answer is not to give another lecture about the value of respect in the workplace, but to examine the calendars and actions of senior leaders. Each of the following bullet points represents an area that the researchers found was directly related to perceptions of respect.

- **Recognize excellence.** Check out your trophy case. How much space is devoted to academic excellence by teachers, students, instructional coaches, paraprofessionals, parents, and others who directly contribute to the achievement of your goals? Do not be surprised at the strong relationship between what each school does well and what it chooses to recognize. One of the least expensive initiatives any school leader can make is to build a few more trophy cases. That, more than anything else, reflects the culture of your schools.

- **Emphasize freedom to use judgment.** Leaders are not micromanagers of the moment, but they are architects of boundaries (Reeves, 2006a). Create a trust index in which you list all the ways—and there are many—in which teachers have the discretion to use their judgment, discretion, and authority. That extensive list stands in stark contrast to the small number of areas in which the senior leadership exerts authority. There are hundreds of ways to teach literature, composition, and geometry, but one cannot choose to avoid teaching literature, composition, and geometry.

- **Listen to and act on teacher ideas.** Would you like to increase your credibility as a leader by many orders of magnitude today? Then take just one idea from a classroom teacher, implement it, give the teacher credit, and watch organizational transformation happen.

- **Encourage innovation.** Many senior leaders are masters of innovation. That's great, and that's a potential limitation. Because when a senior leader is innovative and thoughtful, the impact on the innovative colleagues may be diminished. If you want to encourage teacher leadership, encourage innovation and get out of the way. Consider the advice of Dorothy Leonard and Walter Swap (2005) and create processes that proceed from divergence to convergence.

- **Provide feedback and coaching.** Why did most teachers and administrators enter into the profession of education? Because they were excellent students, good at school, enjoyed school, saw the value in school, in fact *loved* school. Now, however, the same teachers and administrators face students every day who do not share their perspective. They deal with students who find school boring, distasteful, and irrelevant. Some of their students actively hate school. But those disengaged and angry students love something—gang affiliation, social relationships, or brief acknowledgment on the elementary playground or in the high school hallway. When do we provide feedback and coaching? For students, the interval might be every six to nine weeks. For teachers, it might be every one to three years. For administrators, it might be at the end of the year, or it might be at the end of a contract, or it might be never (Reeves, 2004c). If we wish to maximize the power and influence of feedback, then we must provide feedback more frequently at every level—students, teachers, and leaders.

• **Value people as individuals.** This is perhaps the greatest challenge in transforming respect from a song title to a daily reality. It demands that we recognize, as I recently told a colleague who wanted to quit, that "life is short, but relationships are long." Although leaders may see test scores, yearly progress, and interim results as important—and indeed they are—our colleagues may have other priorities, including the birth of a child, the anniversary of a marriage, or the death of a loved one. The power of teacher leadership is seldom more in evidence than when teaching colleagues are more cognizant of these important family events than are senior leaders. One of the bridges that every parent must cross is the acknowledgment that our children have interests that extend beyond our home; wise leaders recognize that colleagues have vital interests and relationships outside of work.

• **Provide a sense of being included.** Putnam (2000) helps us to understand the power of inclusion, and Goleman (2006) suggests that humans and other primates are hardwired for social connection. I have attempted to foster that connection with the Web site www.WikiTeacherLeadership.com and would like to suggest that all system leaders take advantage of this site or create one of their own. What is the worst that could happen? People will say something critical about senior leadership. This is true, and it will be true whether or not you embrace the new framework. Therefore, create multiple initiatives in which to provide a sense of inclusiveness for every colleague. You can listen in person in town meetings and on the Web through forums, discussion boards, and wiki software.

- **Appreciate diverse perspectives, ideas, and work styles.** I admit that if I were king of education, then men would wear bow ties, students would say, "Yes, sir," and parents would display the same reverence for educators I have witnessed in Africa, Asia, and Eastern Europe. However, if I really am interested in embracing a culture of respect, then I must reject fantasies of bygone eras or foreign locales and appreciate diversity. I must consider and appreciate different perspectives, including the parents who will talk with me in a faith community basement, but not in a school. I must embrace the teacher whose clothes and work style are in stark contrast to my own. I must accept the student who challenges me to make school meaningful and relevant. Every challenge and diverse perspective is an opportunity.

- **Encourage full expression of ideas without fear.** "What if we ask them for their advice, and then they actually *tell* us?" The fears of the nervous assistant principal are well founded. When students, teachers, and parents speak, they can speak uncomfortable truths that threaten the prevailing order. Therefore, when senior leaders consider whether or not to encourage full expression without fear, they must assess the relative risk. What is the risk of considering ideas in a public and objective forum? What is the countervailing risk of the same ideas being raised in private and angry forums in which school leaders have neither participation nor any opportunity to provide a countervailing case? For the courageous leader who encourages full expression of ideas without fear, the very worst that will happen is an expression of disagreement that was pervasive anyway. Now, with the encouragement of the leader, this discontent can perhaps be addressed.

- **Listen to and fairly handle complaints.** Fair process, as Kim and Mauborgne (2004) reminded us, does not imply caving in to opposition. Rather, fair process means that leaders must be thoughtful, open, and fair in considering complaints.

Therefore, how do system-level leaders respond to the evidence of systemic change's impact on leaders and teachers? The evidence in Chapter 1 is definitive, as if we needed research to validate common sense: teachers are influenced most by direct observation of the effective practices of other teachers. Therefore, the most effective central office administrators will become the architects of networks in which effective instructional practice is shared in as few degrees of separation as possible. Hierarchy models maximize degrees of separation, as a message spreads from an outside change agent to the superintendent to the deputy to the director to principals to assistant principals to department heads to grade-level leaders to teachers. As with the game of telephone mentioned earlier, in this scenario the message often gets distorted along the way.

State, Provincial, Regional, and County Support for Teacher Leadership

Governments around the world offer a variety of different structures above the local school system. All of the suprasystem levels of governance—counties, states, provinces, regions, and other governmental structures—encounter different labels and complexities, but they all face a strikingly similar challenge: how can they provide support to a variety of complex systems while simultaneously respecting differences and insisting on common values? From the Literacy and Numeracy Secretariat of the Province of Ontario to the Department of Education of the State of California, from the Office of Education of Franklin County, Ohio, to the Boards of Cooperative Education throughout New York and Colorado, the questions and challenges are remarkably similar:

• Our children speak more than 100 languages. How can we possibly expect to put in place a common set of academic standards?
• Our teachers and administrators have developed an exceptional degree of political influence, and this renders change profoundly difficult. How can we expect to implement new policies?

- Our local boards of education and the people who elected them have a deep and abiding belief in local control. How can any regional, provincial, or state authority expect to supersede that?
- System leaders have too many masters. How can any level of government think that it has influence when it is the local level that hires, evaluates, and fires school leaders?

And so it goes. All of the suprasystem levels of educational governance must hold in tension their limitations of power with their profoundly important insights into improving school achievement. California, a unit of government that is far more powerful economically than more than 95 percent of independent countries, offers some interesting insights into the potential of suprasystem levels of educational governance. Bill Habermehl, superintendent of Orange County, California, uses a combination of technology and personal connections to cross the bridge from a system with more than half a million children to the individual 3rd grade classroom. Orange County is a pioneer in the use of interactive video for professional development. Besides public school students, the district also serves a diverse population, including parents whose orthodox Muslim, Jewish, and Christian beliefs require home-schooling for children. "They are *all* our students," Habermehl explained as he proudly displayed his outreach programs giving homeschool, alternative school, and traditional public school students and parents access to the same curriculum, assessment, instruction, and standards.

At the state level, superintendent Doug Christensen in Nebraska has created a remarkable model for teacher empowerment. Perhaps the best reflection of Commissioner Christensen's influence was manifested when I was riding on an exceptionally uncomfortable flight in a middle seat, using all of my psychic energy to keep the plane aloft, while the person in the seat next to me appeared to be intent on grading papers. To take my mind off the turbulence, I inquired, "You must be a teacher. So am I. Do you mind if I ask about your kids?" What followed was one of the most remarkable testimonies to the power of suprasystem educational governance structures I have ever witnessed. My seatmate said, "I've been teaching 8th grade in Grand Island, Nebraska, for 33 years. I thought that I knew what my kids could do, and I thought I was a pretty good teacher. But I just finished some training on scoring, and now the state department has me reading these essays of kids from Scottsbluff, Lincoln, Omaha, and everywhere else, and I'm just astonished. What I used to think was really great is now just pretty good. I never knew that 8th grade kids could do this well. I promise that my 34th year in teaching is going to be better." At this point, we were both in tears. Both of us had taught kids for more than three decades, and we both thought we were more than pretty good teachers. But we had to face the evidence: other teachers who faced the same budgets, contracts, schedules, politics, and leadership were getting better results. We had only two choices—to resent it, or to make our 34th year better than our 33rd year. Commissioner Christensen may not know the impact that he has on education at the classroom level, but when people on turbulent flights to Omaha spend their time focused on student achievement, I think he has more than demonstrated his impact.

Avis Glaze of Ontario province, Canada; Superintendent Patti Harrington of Utah; and Jim Dueck of Alberta Education, Edmonton, Canada, may have never met, but they have all offered insights that are important for the impact of suprasystem leaders. Dr. Dueck and his colleagues have created what I regard as the gold standard of suprasystem research at the Alberta Education Web site (www.education.alberta.ca), where educators around the world can explore how teaching, leadership, curriculum, assessment, and parent involvement affect student achievement. In Ontario, Dr. Glaze must consider her impact on more than 4,000 schools in Ontario province, from some of the world's most successful schools to the most challenged schools. Back in the United States, Dr. Harrington faces a combination of political and demographic challenges. Utah spends fewer dollars per pupil than any state in the United States, yet also produces some of the nation's most successful public schools. She must confront a skeptical legislature and public who quite reasonably ask, "If money is so important, then why does our state continue to produce great students, teachers, and school leaders?" With a combination of self-effacement, grace, professionalism, and modesty, Dr. Harrington is able to acknowledge the impact of local community support for education and challenge citizens and legislators to meet their obligations to every child.

Before Gene Wilhoit assumed the leadership of the Council of Chief State School Officers, he was the chief educational officer of the Commonwealth of Kentucky. Whenever I spoke to a group of Kentucky educators, I was always astonished that Dr. Wilhoit was not positioned on stage, nor did he occupy the typical place of prominence in the front row. On the contrary, Dr. Wilhoit was literally and figuratively on the same side of the table as teachers and school administrators. His willingness to become a learning leader spoke more in actions than I could ever deliver in words.

National Policy Support for Teacher Leadership

For many readers of this book, any discussion of national policy in education smacks of totalitarianism or, at the very least, suggests the beginning of an unpleasant article. The United States is hardly the only culture to express suspicions about the role of the national government in educational policy. In Canada, each province governs its educational system independently; the same is true with each Australian state. China, by contrast, has a unified national educational system. The same is true of many European and African nations. In developing nations that depend on the International Monetary Fund and other sources of aid to survive, national control of the educational system is consistently a requirement, for good or ill. Sometimes national government policies can improve teacher training, student opportunities, and facilities. In other cases, however, centralized structure can be woefully inefficient. In Zambia, for example, there is a surfeit of teachers in some areas where college-trained educators are unemployed and frustrated, yet in other areas the schools suffer from a ratio of 100 students to every teacher and buildings operate in triple shifts, all due to a shortage of teachers that is local, but not national. Given the wide divergence of philosophies globally about the role of the national government in education, the challenge of making any coherent recommendations can be daunting. Nevertheless, because networks of teacher leaders will exist whether or not the national government participates in the movement, leaders should be aware of ways that national governments can enhance these networks without undermining their culture and traditions in educational policy.

First, national governments can stimulate research and disseminate it widely. As noted earlier, Alberta Education has done a masterful job of accumulating research not only on student test scores but also on specific actions in schools that are related to test scores. Casting a wide net, the research interests of Alberta Education (formerly Alberta Learning) include programs not only for academic achievement but also for student engagement, discipline, behavior, parent involvement, and a host of other vital research questions. This Web site is particularly useful for teachers and researchers in the field of second-language and native nation (in Canada, First Nations) studies. In the United States, the What Works Clearinghouse Web site is a treasure trove of research on the impact (and more commonly, on the lack of impact) of many instructional programs. In addition to stimulating and reporting on research, the What Works Clearinghouse establishes standards for educational research and reporting so that readers can determine whether a conclusion is based on a single case study or a larger sample. Australia, with its wide variation in population concentrations, offers particular insight into the possibilities and pitfalls of distance learning and the challenges associated with educating students from a bewildering array of backgrounds. Links to these and other research sites can be found at www.WikiTeacherLeadership.com.

Second, national governments can commit to evidence-based educational decisions, at least with respect to the projects that they support with funding. Although this may seem obvious—what else would we do except make decisions based on evidence?—the plain fact is that the criteria for decision making can range from folklore to self-dealing by policymakers. Although national governments will never supplant local decision making, central governments can create an environment in which research and evidence have a greater influence on educational policy.

Third, broaden the research perspective at the national level to include action research by teachers. The standards of research at the national level typically emphasize the gold standard of random assignment of research subjects to experimental and control groups and carefully controlled research conditions. In order to gain the label of "large" or "moderate" evidence to support a claim, the What Works Clearinghouse (U.S. Department of Education, 2002) requires that the research include more than one study and more than one school, and that the sample size include at least 350 students. The text of the No Child Left Behind Act refers to "scientifically based research" more than 200 times. Other national educational governing organizations around the world also establish research standards that focus on large-scale quantitative methods of experimental inquiry. Certainly, action research by networks of teachers is not a substitute for these formal studies, but action research can be an important complement to other methods. If national governments would extend their research umbrella to include action research projects, then government advocates of evidence-based educational decision making could anticipate the question, "But will it really work here?" and point to a multitude of small and inexpensive action research projects by working educators. Educational reform history is littered with programs that had a solid claim to scientific support but were imposed in a hierarchical manner and never adopted with full fidelity at the classroom level. If teachers were part of the research team rather than mere recipients of research conducted by others, it is possible that the subsequent large-scale implementation of educational reforms could have been more successful. When action research becomes part of the national research methodology, there will inevitably be bridges built between researchers and practitioners. Without those bridges, there is a chasm of cynicism and distrust that undermines even the best research-based programs.

Fourth, national governments can facilitate an exchange of ideas, teachers, research, and practice within the country and among many other countries. Imagine a "national science fair" in which teachers share their most effective practices and learn from colleagues who have faced similar challenges but engaged in strikingly different strategies. The national government can therefore become the architect and facilitator of an international network of teacher leadership and learning.

The Next Chapters

Who will write the next chapters of *Reframing Teacher Leadership to Improve Your School?* You will, along with your colleagues around the world. The noncommercial Web site www.WikiTeacherLeadership.com will include the ideas, dialogues, practices, debates, and action research projects of teachers around the world. The new framework is, after all, a continual process in which resilience leads to an enhanced capacity for generating additional questions, challenges, and research. If you are fortunate enough to work in a resilient environment, then share your success stories. If you are suffering in the context of the fact-free debate, then explore the ideas of your colleagues who have managed to change their course away from the path of rejection and diminished capacity. I implore you to act now. Do not wait to be invited to become a teacher leader. Do not wait for an officially sanctioned action research project. Do not wait for an official policy or negotiated agreement to create, in excruciating detail, a set of burdensome definitions and limits on teacher leadership. Whatever the labels and language, whatever your position, you are a teacher leader right now. The only questions are whether you use your ability as a teacher leader to engage in the most provocative challenges of our profession, whether you will share your findings publicly, and whether you will use the teacher leader platform locally and on the Internet to engage in an unending journey of leadership and learning. Whatever your present circumstances, you can join a network of colleagues committed to exploring teaching leadership and expanding the influence of the new framework. I will be with you on that journey.

APPENDIX A

ACTION RESEARCH WRITTEN REPORTS FOR CLARK COUNTY SCHOOL DISTRICT, NEVADA, MAY 2007

Team: Jill Cribari and Barrie Kraft

Question: How has the implementation of Step Up to Writing influenced writing instruction and student scores on the State Writing Proficiency Examination at Detwiler Elementary School?

Abstract: Detwiler Elementary School focused attention on increasing student proficiency on the Nevada State Writing Proficiency Exam. An organizational-based writing program, Step Up to Writing, was implemented in grades 1–5 in an effort to strengthen student writing. Evaluators looked at schoolwide scores for the past three years and compared proficiency rates. Though scores have increased every year, it is not possible to attribute increases solely to the implementation of Step Up to Writing. Other possible influences include after-school tutoring, classroom instruction, and pullout instruction. Because of a significant increase in proficiency in the area of organization, we feel it is worthwhile to maintain and improve the use of Step Up to Writing.

Team: Jeanine Tegano

Question: Moving thoughts and dancing words: Charting changes in student understanding and articulation of dance compositions

Abstract: As a second-year teacher in the Clark County School District, I have engaged in ongoing coursework and professional development in my discipline of dance in concert with refining and reflecting on educational pedagogy and juggling the demands of classroom teaching with the after-school rehearsal and production demands of a performing arts educator. My training as a teacher was in the field of history, and the results of a rigorous graduate experience that gave equal weight to content and pedagogy yielded a particular kind of thinking in terms of understanding the word "effective" in the context of "effective education." With one eye on the discipline and the other eye on the pedagogy, I was constantly challenged to fuse the two. When I entered the classroom as a dance educator, the same kind of question was at the forefront of my mind: how can I engage my students to learn dance through methodologies that actually involve them practicing the intellectual and physical skills of a dancer/choreographer, authentically at their level? Through my ongoing coursework, open professional dance classes, and professional development workshops, I have continued to expand and refine what it means to move, think, respond, and choreograph as a dancer. Now my challenge is to layer these practices into the way I teach and how I want my students to learn. I have considered the quality of work that is inherent in my own training as a dance student, and I have used that knowledge to inform the kinds of work I would like my students to produce, the kind of thinking processes I would like for them to encounter as they ultimately produce that work. Therefore, I am curious about the following questions: What is the best way to teach the physical and intellectual skills of dance to beginning students? How do we get students to think and produce as choreographers? What is the best way to teach content so that the knowledge becomes a part of who the students are?

Team: Tamara White

Question: Does the incorporation of Howard Gardner's Multiple Intelligence Theory (MIT) in mathematics lesson planning and delivery improve student retention of taught curriculum?

Abstract: Mojave High School (MHS), situated in North Las Vegas, Nevada, is located in the Northeast Region of the Clark County School District. The school opened in 1996 for students in grades 9–12. Current enrollment is 2,340 students, with 49 percent female and 51 percent male students. The ethnic analysis of the student population reveals that MHS is 68.5 percent minority. This percentage reflects an increase in the Hispanic and African American student population as documented

in the last three years. Currently 31 percent of students at MHS participate in the free and reduced-price lunch program. Limited-English-
proficiency students represent 10 percent of the student population, and
students receiving services through an individualized educational plan
(IEP) represent 14 percent of the overall population. For the second
year, MHS has been classified as a school in need of improvement based
on adequate yearly progress (AYP) criteria of No Child Left Behind.
Nevada uses the Nevada High School Proficiency Examination
(NHSPE) to measure student achievement. Improvement strategies at
MHS are aimed at elevating the mathematics and reading scores for students, particularly those who are members of a minority group. Data
from the 2004–2005 school year show that students are not meeting
standards in mathematics and reading. This number increases when you
reference data on African American and Hispanic students. Administrative and regional efforts for MHS are directed at increasing the number
of proficient students, thereby increasing the number of students who
graduate with all requirements fulfilled by the end of their four-year tenure in high school. The MHS School Improvement Plan (SIP) has several goals related to improving student achievement on the NHSPE in
an effort to address AYP status. Goal 1 and Goal 2 specifically cite the
elevation of overall mathematics and reading scores on the NHSPE.
Goal 1 states, "MHS will successfully meet AYP or Safe Harbor requirements for each of the eight subgroups in English Language Arts as determined by student achievement on the NHSPE." Goal 2 states, "MHS
will successfully meet AYP or Safe Harbor requirements for each of the
eight subgroups in mathematics as determined by student achievement
on the NHSPE" (SIP, 2005).

Team: Gretchen Vineyard
Question: How do teachers perceive the role of the education computing specialist?
Abstract: This study is about the practice of an education computing
specialist (ECS) who works at two schools, which include three campuses

within the Clark County School District (CCSD). The ECS is a technology coordinator who responds to the technical problems of staff and students, totaling 429 people. She also maintains 257 computers and 160 printers and administers the fully networked schools. The ECS position began in 1997 to help teachers integrate technology into the curriculum. Although helping teachers add supporting technology to classroom lessons impacts student achievement, this part of the job does not take place often enough because of the time the technical aspect of the job demands. This time imbalance is a focus of the study. Three surveys of the teaching staff reveal that teachers perceive the ECS primarily as a technician, although she is a licensed teacher with a master's degree in technology in education. This matter of how the time is spent is complex, as these schools have the latest technology and with ECS help could more strategically use technology as a tool to build student achievement; instead, time is spent on technical support to keep everything running. Twenty-eight teachers participated in a survey, seven of whom became part of a larger study with the ECS as she conducted a method of integrating technology. Gathering data after working with these teachers was another part of the study. The results of that action demonstrate that when the ECS worked with teachers to enhance their lessons, modeling how the technology was taught with their students, teachers' attitudes about attempting the same lessons using like technology were positive.

Team: Rosie Perez
Question: How do parent involvement and home literacy experiences facilitate emergent literacy development in kindergarten students?
Abstract: From January 2007 through May 2007, I studied how the lack of parent involvement hindered the emergent literacy development of my students, as there was not a home-school connection or home literacy experiences upon which a foundation could be built to facilitate student achievement in 18 at-risk kindergarten students. After parents participated in parent-child monthly bilingual meetings, parents were

encouraged to become active participants in their child's schooling, learn the importance of reading to their child, and gain an understanding of standards and benchmarks their child was expected to master by the end of kindergarten. Post-test results provided evidence that the meetings positively affected parent involvement and, in turn, achievement and growth in my students' emergent literacy development soared. In particular, I looked at student growth in the areas of letter recognition, letter-sounds, rhyme, initial sound fluency, and phoneme segmentation. Data were collected using pre- and post-tests, including the Phonological Awareness Literacy Screening-K (PALS-K) and Dynamic Indicators of Basic Early Literacy Skills-K (DIBELS-K) assessments. These data were averaged to determine the mean for the class aside from the English language learner (ELL) subgroup.

Team: Mike Scudder

Question: How does mastery of the fundamental math skills of addition, subtraction, multiplication, and division affect math achievement in middle school?

Abstract: From January 22, 2007, until May 5, 2007, I monitored and evaluated one 6th grade, one 7th grade, and one 8th grade math class at Von Tobel Middle School on their fundamental math skills of addition, subtraction, multiplication, and division. I administered a pretest of 60 questions (15 each of addition, subtraction, multiplication, and division). I then had 10 to 15 minutes of warm-up on the four math fundamentals at the beginning of each class. I covered approximately three weeks of addition, three weeks of subtraction, three weeks of multiplication, and three weeks of division. I used the FlashMaster Computer for the classes. Finally, I gave a post-test covering the same questions as the pre-test. The post-test results and the comparison of 3rd- and 4th-quarter grades support positively that the higher degree of expertise on the fundamental math facts increases achievement in middle school and offers an increase in potential future achievement in mathematics.

Team: Hanna Fletcher

Question: Multicultural literature and the development of a reading identity among African American students

Abstract: Francis H. Cortney Junior High's School Improvement Plan (SIP) seeks to address the needs of our diverse student population, and of critical importance is the literacy development of our African American students. Of the African American students, 85.7 percent scored below proficiency level on the 2006 8th grade Reading Criterion-Referenced Test (CRT). The lowest reading test scores were from the strands of developing an interpretation; reading to comprehend, interpret, and evaluate informational text; and reading to comprehend, interpret, and evaluate literature. From February 2007 through May 2007, I tracked the development of a "reading identity" among culturally diverse students participating in my 7th grade multicultural literature elective course. My research focused on the relationship between students' views of reading, their use of reading strategies, and their levels of academic engagement when exposed to culturally diverse literature and curriculum. In particular, I examined whether the inclusion of multicultural literature and culturally responsive curriculum helped cultivate a reading identity among African American students as evidenced by increased literacy development, reading engagement, and confidence as readers.

Team: Sylvia A. Johnson, MEd

Question: Reading with applicable practice

Abstract: From January 2007 to May 2007, this teacher studied students' daily silent reading choices with relation to students' participation, motivation for choice reading, and increased self-confidence to read trade books of various genres. Fifteen to 17 students participated in the SSR daily and wrote a Quickie Book Report (QBR), a method used to verify actual reading happening at the appointed sustained silent reading time. In particular, she specially selected and shelved in the classroom library for students' choice reading the trade books modeled in the textbook to determine if students' choices boosted gains in reading success.

A comprehension pre-test/post-test was administered to determine if choice readings of selected trade books confidently affected gains in students' comprehension of text. The researcher daily performed a read-aloud to establish successful reading strategies for students in a nonthreatening method. An interview conducted with each participant gave insightful viewpoints from the learners' thoughts on the trade book versus the textbook. Most students preferred reading the smaller trade book version of the story. Read-aloud influenced most students in their choice time readings, signifying that successful reading strategies can contribute to choice reading time participation. Students compiled a student's choice vocabulary book, Reading Vocabulary Dictionary (RVD), from literature read during the designated sustained silent reading (SSR) times. Field notes kept throughout this study listed a log of the books students read, a listing of read-aloud books, and details of this teacher's practices. Teacher's reflections and students' interview responses suggested that these practices—SSR, QBR, RVD, and read-aloud—can easily continue adding practice for students in successful reading strategies.

Team: Raquel H. Gutherie and Janelle K. Neuman
Question: Use of the matrix for articulating instructional objectives to facilitate diverse learners' achievement across academic domains
Abstract: Use of the matrix for articulating instructional objectives in the development and presentation of curriculum across the academic domains examines the theory that students who are exposed to higher-order thinking skills and open-ended questioning strategies demonstrate increased academic achievement and assessment scores. Research indicates that development of student cognitive capabilities can produce the substantial academic and social growth needed to reduce the learning gap for at-risk children. The goal of this study was to examine how, and to what degree, the use of the matrix for articulating instructional objectives based on the revised Bloom's taxonomy would improve diverse learners' academic achievement. The study was conducted with a group of 17 3rd grade students and their teacher. Achievement data collection

was measured using the following: student and teacher interviews; parent, teacher, and student surveys; examination of frequency of matrix use in teacher lesson plans; classroom observations of instructional strategies and student responses; evaluation of teacher questions and student responses; examination of student response journals; and examination of semester grades and assessment reports. Our preliminary results suggest that the use of the matrix may have contributed to an increase in student achievement; however, use of the matrix alone in lesson plan development did not result in a measurable change in teacher questioning behaviors during lesson delivery.

Team: Nancy O. Navarro-Agustin and Jalene Pardo
Question: Does teaching parents strategies they can implement at home to teach their children how to read produce an improvement in reading ability of students with reading delays?

Abstract: We asked teachers from kindergarten to 3rd grade to identify students from their classroom who scored 60 percent and under in reading on the school district's second trimester interim assessments. These assessments classify these students as below grade level in language arts. We juxtaposed interim assessment results with scores in the DIBELS assessment results to ensure and confirm deficiency in reading skills. There were 129 students identified from the school population of 850. In compliance with existing statutes on confidentiality of student data, teachers provided the researcher only the number of students in their classroom who qualified for the study. This researcher provided teachers with recruitment letters to invite identified parents to attend a weekly workshop where they could learn literacy strategies they could use to enhance activities they already did at home. The teachers sent the letters home to the parents of the identified students. There were 12 responses received; one of them answered no. The week before the start of the workshop, we invited all 129 parents again to attend a meeting where we explained the benefits for attending the workshop. On the day of the meeting, the same 11 respondents came. All the respondents were

ELLs, some of whom have only been in the country for a few months and whose children scored 0 on the assessments. The workshop started with these 11 parents. The curriculum had two modules: learning English, facilitated by the ELL specialist; and learning literacy strategies, facilitated by this researcher. The ELL specialist facilitated the first session, focusing on vocabulary. This researcher facilitated the second module and explained and modeled the strategies, and parents practiced them. We created or supplied to the parents the materials necessary to implement the strategies at home. Each week, the number of attendees varied, and there were six parents whose attendance was fairly constant. (These are the parents of students A, B, C, D, E, and F, whose test results are included in the report.) We modeled literacy strategies based on a balanced program with focus on skills to acquire phonological awareness, reading vocabulary including sight words and high-frequency words, vocabulary that focused on word meanings and usage, reading fluency, and comprehension. We sat at a table, and each session began with a review of last session's strategies and then discussions on what parents did at home when a child exhibited difficulties on a specific skill—the topic of the day's lesson. As each parent talked, others interjected, offered problems, gave suggestions, and made positive comments. The researcher acknowledged all the parents and their techniques, then modeled enhancements, adding techniques as necessary. Parents practiced activities with the facilitators. We reviewed, repeated, and redirected as necessary. Each participant represented what they learned in a journal, through notes or illustrations that helped them understand and remember when they used the strategies at home. Each session began with a review of past strategies and ended also with a review of the strategies learned that day. This researcher made sure to end each session with positive feedback to each parent, praising them for their efforts and desire to help their children. The ELL specialist delivered and translated each lesson, each strategy, and each sentence to ensure the parents understood specifically the complexity and the nuances of the English language.

Team: Brad Patrick Daughtry and Donna Holland

Question: Does the direct teaching of metacognitive strategies impact student achievement in reading?

Abstract: From November 2006 through June 2007, we studied the relationship between metacognitive strategies and achievement in reading. We examined the concept of teaching metacognitive strategies isolated from the language arts block of instruction. The strategies were isolated from daily reading instruction and assessed separately from the daily reading block. Reading achievement was measured for this report using five reading strategies, five pre-assessments, five post-assessments, and standardized test scores. Two classes were used in this research. Class A was a 5th grade class comprising primarily ELLs. There was also one student who had been identified as learning disabled in the area of math. Class B was a 5th grade class and also comprised primarily ELLs. There was one student who had been identified as learning disabled in language arts and math. Data collection will continue through the end of the trimester using state tests, information that is not available at this time. In addition, the teaching of the strategies was expanded to 3rd grade to see if the teaching of these strategies would positively affect reading performance. The 3rd grade class consisted of 15 students. Twelve of the students spoke Spanish as their first language, and two were special education students. The teacher of the 3rd grade class has completed two years of teaching elementary school. Preliminary findings suggest that teaching metacognitive strategies separately results in substantial gains in student performance on reading assessments.

Team: Victoria Norby

Question: How to transition students' written responses to literature from personal to critical analysis

Abstract: From August 2007 through May 2007, this teacher studied the impact of teaching students critical thinking, reading, and writing strategies to determine if their deeper understanding of the texts would create higher achievement on standardized test scores and at the same time build strategies that would benefit the students in higher education. Implemented was a three-phase plan that began with the building of a community of learners; interventions were then put in place to raise the expectations of analysis versus multiple-choice or short-answer assessments, and the final phase moved the class from teacher-directed to student-driven instruction. At the conclusion of the final phase, narrative interviews were conducted online with the 19 subject participants; online surveys were delivered to the subjects of the study, to teachers, and to students outside the study in the 10th grade English classes. The results from the study seem to indicate that once students have mastered test-taking strategies, we must teach higher levels of Bloom's taxonomy to develop students no longer in need of remediation at the college level. Teacher and student surveys do not indicate a unified understanding of the concepts or importance of critical thinking, reading, and writing. Throughout the year, the teacher was able to move her students from delivering the answer they thought the teacher wanted to hear to a classroom full of learners who were questing for the deeper meanings of the curriculum.

Team: Kassie DeLaSalle

Question: How does the use of pocket charts and personal readers for skill and strategy instruction through poetry, songs, fingerplays, and letter and word sorts facilitate the development of emergent literacy skills in at-risk prekindergarten students?

Abstract: From January 2007 through April 2007, I studied how using pocket charts and personal readers for skill and strategy instruction through poetry, songs, fingerplays, and letter/word sorts facilitated the development of emergent literacy skills in 26 at-risk prekindergarten students. In particular, I looked at student growth in the areas of letter recognition, vocabulary, rhyme, alliteration, and concept of print and word. Data was collected using pre- and post-tests, including the PALS-PreK Assessment for Letter Recognition; the Get It, Got It, Go! Assessment for Vocabulary, Rhyme, and Alliteration; and the PALS-PreK Assessment for Concept of Print/Word. These data were averaged to determine the mean for the class as a whole, for male and female subgroups, and for the ELL subgroup. Students participated in whole-group instruction each day on skills and strategies that support emergent literacy development in the areas of phonemic awareness, letter-sound relationships/phonics, concepts of print and word, vocabulary, fluency, and motivation through the use of pocket charts containing poetry, songs, fingerplays, and letter and word sorts; lesson extensions for small-group instruction using personal readers containing copies of pocket chart material to reinforce and practice skills and strategies; and differentiated instruction that addressed individual student needs. Post-test results provided evidence that the use of pocket charts and personal readers positively affects the development of at-risk prekindergarten students' emergent literacy skills.

Team: Erica Bender, EdM
Question: Does participation in scholastic chess affect student achievement?
Abstract: A growing body of research indicates that involvement in scholastic chess has a positive influence on student achievement. Achievement that is congruent with a child's potential is the goal that excellent educators strive to cultivate in each student. Achievement is "the attainment or accomplishment of something noteworthy [by a student] after much effort and often in spite of obstacles and discouragements" (*Merriam-Webster's Online Dictionary*). School counselors have the unique professional responsibility of taking a holistic view of student achievement. CCSD school counseling focuses on three distinct domains that are designed to promote the growth and development of the whole child. These three areas of concentration include the academic domain, the personal-social domain, and the career exploration domain. If considered separately, the latter is an extension of both the academic and personal-social domains. Therefore, for the purposes of this project, and for this report, student achievement is viewed as growth, development, or attainment of students in either the academic

or the personal-social realm, or both. An evaluation of the effect of chess education on academic progress by Paradise Professional Development School (K–5, hereafter PPDS) was made by examining mathematics grades of participants over the course of the school year. From a counseling perspective, development in the personal-social domain is a critical component of student achievement. More attention was given to the analysis of the influences of chess education on the personal-social domain than the academic domain. Levels of involvement and engagement are measured by participation and attendance records and teacher and parent surveys. The data were derived from a combination of quantitative and qualitative information.

Team: Gale Mendes and Nathan Webster
Question: Is there a relationship between both non-IEP and IEP students having the opportunity to make assignment and activity choices and their academic achievement in class?
Abstract: During the 2006–2007 school year, my action research project examined the possible relationship between students having the opportunity to choose their assignments for each unit of study and their overall academic achievement in their World Geography class. In order to obtain my results, I tallied not only all the activities each of the students chose for Units 2–10, but also the unit grade each student received as well as the grade received on two exams. I compared the scores of the non-IEP students with those of the IEP students. For the IEP students in Period A, the findings indicate there was a moderate positive relationship between the grade the IEP students received on their units of study and the grade they received on their exams. In Period B, the data show the non-IEP students demonstrated a moderate positive relationship between the grade they received on their units of study and their exam grades. It is, however, important to note that the data for both Period A IEP students and Period B non-IEP students do not indicate a strong relationship between the grades students received on their units of study and their exam grades. I also looked closely at the vocabulary choice

activities to see if there was one that was more popular than another. The data indicate that for both IEP and non-IEP students in both Periods A and B the favorite vocabulary activity choice was the illustrated dictionary entry. My coteacher and I have reflected on the results of this study and have been able to discern important information that will help us to plan for next year.

Team: Patrick Jacobson

Question: Does an extreme emphasis toward the teaching of math and understanding of math facts—addition, subtraction, multiplication, and division—have a relationship to success on IDMS tests and other standardized tests?

Abstract: In an article written in *Shoptalk* by David Thiel in the CCSD Regional Professional Development Program secondary math department, he said students need to learn math facts like they know their name. In the article, it is stated that this math fluency enables them to increase their achievement. This study set out to find if this is so. From October 2006 to March 2007, I studied how students learn math facts in my classroom and gathered information from other teachers about how they teach and reinforce math facts. I also gathered information and data to indicate the achievement levels attained and how they relate to scores on district Instructional Data Management System (IDMS) tests, as well as CRTs. Math facts achievement was measured through the use of randomized 100-question tests. They consisted of multiplication, addition, and subtraction tests; students were given five minutes to complete each test. In each instance, the first trimester interim test and the second trimester interim test coincided with the administration of the facts tests. The facts tests were added together for a possible score of 300, and then the score on all three was averaged to get a percentage. I then ran a statistical test to determine if there was any relation to the facts scores and scores on the interim tests math score percentage. The individuals included in this study consisted of 126 3rd grade students at Bonner Elementary School. At this point, results indicate there is a positive relationship between math facts knowledge and the results of the interim tests. I am currently awaiting the results of the spring CRTs, and will add them to the body of this report when they are available.

Team: Ty Jackson
Question: The effect of character education on the behavior of 8th grade male students
Abstract: The research question that I'm trying to answer in this project is if character education lessons in health class affect 8th grade boys' behavior in school. The behaviors that will be focused on are the discipline of students on campus as well as the influence on the completion of homework. The term "character education" is very broad, and I will narrow the focus to a couple key areas. I'm going to focus my attention on responsibility, trust, commitment, and self-awareness. All of these various characteristics are subjective in nature and controlled by the individual person. I currently have three 8th grade boys' health classes and am going to compare one class, my character group, to the other two classes, noncharacter group. My character group will be receiving the "character education" lessons, the treatment, approximately once per week, and the noncharacter group will not be receiving the lessons. The variables to be measured are going to have various components, including the school problems inventory, homework completion, anecdotal records, and student view survey. First, we are going to track the average number of incomplete, late, and missing assignments for each group. Another academic variable will consist of class averages for individual assignments as well as the overall average. Additional discipline behaviors will be tracked in conjunction with the Dean of Students office. I will compare the number of discipline referrals for students within each group. The subcategories will consist of suspensions, expulsions, and students sent to behavior schools. I will take the average number for the noncharacter group and compare to the number for the character group. Lastly, I'm going to survey the students and ask them their thoughts and

feelings in regard to the character education program. Once students have completed the surveys, the results will be compiled to gauge the students' views of the effectiveness of the character education lessons. Furthermore, in life, to have success you need to commit to a philosophy or school of thought. They have to trust, wholeheartedly, in what the leader believes in and their perspective. Leaders need to be positive role models and live what they teach on a daily basis. By displaying these desirable character traits, students will experience what it takes to be successful. Complete honesty with students will be openly communicated. Verbal communication will be a method of translating success and failures, along with written communication on weekly goals. Weekly updates and clear expectations of class averages will be a method of communicating current academic status. Student behavior expectations will be displayed in percentages of 8th grade male students compared to the entire student population.

Team: Mary Schumacher and Amanda LaTurner
Question: How do setting goals and the use of differentiated instruction influence student achievement, attitudes, and perceptions towards mathematics?
Abstract: My colleague and I were looking for a way to motivate 4th and 5th grade students to really care about their math work and improve their attitude toward understanding math in general. We have not been completely satisfied with any one particular math program, but used the programs outlined by our district along with our grade-level benchmarks to set goals for each class. As we began to do diagnostic testing, we realized that low CRT test scores from the previous year were probably more accurate than we had hoped. Too many students were not ready for grade-level concepts; they needed more practice and review in true number sense. When teaching the whole group, we seemed to get a lot of glazed looks during direct instruction and class discussions, not to mention all the incomplete or inaccurate practice worksheets that were not being turned in. So many students were

not catching on and didn't seem to be bothered by the fact that they were getting further and further behind. In my 20 years of teaching and the 8 years of my colleague, we had never seen such apathy in such a high percentage of students. We needed to do something to make these students care about learning, so we had our students fill out a math survey to help us determine how they felt about math so we might better know how to address their needs. Our survey analysis led us to believe that we needed small-group intervention for students who weren't getting those basic concepts we were teaching or reviewing on a weekly basis. We also decided to set goals for each individual student and conference with each student at least once a week on his or her progress. We then used a standard electronic diagnostic test with all students to track their progress. Once each student was assessed, we assigned math homework on his or her own level. We continued to move through grade-level benchmarks as a whole group with practice and review from the grade-level materials to help them be more prepared for end-of-year testing. Homework, however, was practicing the same objectives at the level they could comprehend. In giving students work they could actually comprehend and finish on their own, we seemed to be getting more accurately finished products actually turned in. Our findings indicate that setting goals and offering differentiated instruction do produce a more positive outcome where math is concerned, in student achievement as well as attitude.

Team: Carol Lynn
Question: Does a school-designed after-school program have a positive impact on students' academic performance?
Abstract: This study was designed to determine the effectiveness of custom-designing an after-school program. The program in this school had been constructed by faculty for the past several years on the basis of a combination of student needs and faculty interests. All of the course offerings were supported by school budget funds or district grant funds. All of the necessary paperwork was always submitted, but an actual study

of the program effectiveness was never conducted. The current climate of accountability has made a study of this program a timely project. Our offerings after school are varied, but I chose to concentrate on four of the activities: Chess Club, Homework Club, Compass Learning, and Extended Day Academy. The overall attendance in these programs totaled 120 students. From this enrollment, I randomly chose 79 students to follow. In this group of 79 are 11 students who participated in multiple activities. Data collection will be through attendance rosters, standardized test scores, and classroom records. This would be accomplished through routine communication with teachers and the use of the IDMS capabilities. Preliminary findings disclosed some interesting facts. Out of the examination of 158 academic performances in reading and math, there were more positive changes in the area of reading, there was an almost equal split in math between the positive and negative changes, and the most effective seemed to be the Homework Club. The least effective seemed to be the Chess Club.

Team: Jason Kern

Question: Can guest speakers increase motivation of at-risk seniors?

Abstract: From September 2006 thorough May 2007, I invited guest speakers into two English IV co-op classrooms in an attempt to improve motivation. I selected speakers from a variety of community resources, including various recruiters, motivational speakers, professionals, technical colleges, and junior colleges and universities. I interviewed and observed the students before and after the speakers, often tailoring the next speaker to the classes' needs. Data collection involved comparing the speaker surveys from the various survey types, a teacher journal documenting anecdotal data on classroom behavior, and other motivational markers such as attendance and homework attempted and completed. My findings suggest the best speakers for these students are the job- or career-related speakers, whose effects lasted longer than the other types of speakers.

Team: Samantha Hager

Question: Positive behavior support team interventions: Effects on perception of safety and student academic performance

Abstract: During the 2006–2007 school year, the effects of a schoolwide positive behavior support program were studied. Interventions were begun specifically on the playground to attempt to help students feel safer and increase structure for staff members during playground duty times. A survey was given in the fall of 2006 and in the spring of 2007 to assess the effectiveness of the interventions. In addition, two 3rd grade classes and one 5th grade class were surveyed to determine academic preference and perceptions of safety. These were then linked to the interim assessment exam.

Team: Gia Moore

Question: The impact of knowledge, self-efficacy, and test anxiety through the lens of the standardized exam

Abstract: Over the past year, Rancho High School has faced a multitude of different challenges pertaining to the obligations of the No Child Left Behind legislation. Given the added pressures of this legislation, accountability measures have been based substantially on student performance on standardized exams. Several measures have been taken to address site-specific issues surrounding Rancho High School. Rancho is currently in its third year of "needs improvement" status. Because of this, the school improvement team made a collaborative decision to target students who had the most probable chance of succeeding in passing these crucial assessments. This research involved the identification and support of nonproficient 11th grade students. The students that were selected for participation in this project were approaching proficiency status, or in other words, close to passing. Therefore, it was hypothesized that additional support targeting proficiency test content and test-taking skills would provide students with the knowledge necessary to pass the exams. The students who were selected for this project did not pass the reading or mathematics proficiency exams or both. Additionally, they were selected because of their projected ability to pass the exams and because they are representative of underserved populations. One of the primary goals of this project was to close the achievement gap and attend to students that are typically overrepresented in dropout populations. Our ultimate goal throughout the duration of this research project was to provide support for the students to pass the HSPE and graduate from high school, while developing a model for meeting the needs of at-risk populations.

Team: Dr. Jodet-Marie Harris
Question: The guiding light: Using guided notes to enhance academic skills of students with learning disabilities
Abstract: This study evaluated the effects of guided notes on the performance of students with learning disabilities during a social studies class. Two students with mild disabilities participated in this study during the third quarter of their social studies class. Measures included achievement on quizzes and tests, class participation, ability to write higher-order thinking questions, summarization skills, and student satisfaction with the procedure. Findings indicate that guided notes had an impact on students' achievement. Recommendations for program development and future research were made.

Team: Nicole E. Klimow, MEd
Question: Will literacy proficiency improve for longtime ELLs placed in an intensive Title I literacy class in addition to their core literacy class?
Abstract: Title I–funded reading and writing programs assist schools with large disadvantaged populations in meeting the needs of at-risk learners and closing achievement gaps. The purpose of this study was to determine whether longtime ELL students enrolled in a Title I–funded intensive literacy class, in addition to their district-funded reading and writing classes, will improve their literacy proficiency and, possibly, gain parity with their counterparts who are not second-language learners.

Using a comparable mock writing test as a pre-test and the Nevada Writing Proficiency Test administered in the spring as a post-test, a pre- and post-diagnostic reading inventory, and interviews and field notes, we examined achievement, perception, and attendance data to determine whether the additional literacy class accelerated literacy proficiency for longtime ELLs. Results of the study suggest that, in fact, the additional literacy class improved literacy development in our longtime ELL students. To understand better why the longtime ELLs succeeded in this model, future study is needed to examine more closely the relationship of instructional practice and placement in the intensive literacy class. Eventually, we want to identify strategies and practices within the Intensive Literacy classes that lead to increased student performance that could be recommended for adoption in similar settings elsewhere in CCSD.

Team: Tresa Harrell
Question: How does reflective practice (keeping journals) impact student academic achievement regarding work internships in grades 10, 11, and 12?
Abstract: We hypothesized that the amount of communication between the advisor, the intern, and his or her employer/supervisor would correlate positively and significantly with attendance and student academic successes within the internship program. Our central hypothesis proposed that higher advisor ratings on all six subcharacteristics (e.g., background, task-oriented skills) would correlate significantly with intern satisfaction ratings, employment activity, and student participation such that more favorable leadership ratings would be associated with higher intern satisfaction, more employment activity, more student participation, and better attendance.

Team: Cynthia Rice
Question: Does an action service–learning project on campus beautification increase connectedness to school and graduation for seniors?

Abstract: From September 2006 through March 2007, I studied the relationship between completing an action service–learning project on campus beautification and connectedness to school and graduation for seniors. In particular, 140 seniors at Silverado High School in the Smart Grad Program selected a mentor that had meaning for them on campus. They then created their own three-hour action service–learning project that focused on campus beautification. They completed the project while checking in with their mentor during the process. A pre- and post-questionnaire was given to the seniors with 20 questions focusing on four areas: school connectedness, resiliency/self-esteem, graduation and academic learning, and the importance of mentors. There was also a pre- and post-questionnaire given to the mentors. The preliminary findings suggest that there were individual and group gains in the importance of all areas for the students and the mentors after the service-learning project, but there are still other factors to be considered. Overall, the response and feedback were very positive, and this was a sample group to test with the intention of expanding the service-learning project and mentoring program to the entire senior class and then schoolwide.

Team: Jennifer N. Guyer

Question: The impact of creative writing on school connectedness and achievement

Abstract: Students participated in academic and fine arts enrichment academies during track breaks. Roberta C. Cartwright students participated in a year-round school, track five pilot program in which camps were offered between track breaks. Specialists were encouraged to develop unique and interesting programs to engage and connect students to their school. This action research project surveyed students who participated in the enrichment academy titled Books for Uganda! Students who participated engaged in creative writing assignments that would be edited, published, and printed in order to donate them to children living in Uganda, Africa. The enrichment academy served as an academic and community service–based project. Students were surveyed before and after the project. Their opinions about school, writing, and culture were collected and compared to determine the impact of the enrichment academy. Findings suggest that school connectedness, interest in making books, writing for fun, and learning about Africa increased. Student confidence in writing skills and interest in writing seemed to decrease. Interest in traveling to Africa and volunteering/donating decreased. These results raise questions about how students define their skill level.

Team: Cathy DeFresne
Question: Using the lesson study model of professional development to enhance teacher collaboration
Abstract: This study examines the effects of the formal lesson study model of professional development to enhance the quality of teacher collaboration time. Current professional development is of a top-down nature in which teachers have little or no control over the structures of their professional development opportunities. The purpose of this study is to address the gap between the school improvement plan's goal of providing adequate professional development time and the actual amount of time that teachers are given to collaborate on, synthesize, and implement new strategies. In this study, teachers from different content areas will form study teams utilizing the lesson study format. These experimental groups will be observed, videotaped, and surveyed in order to determine if there is a significant difference in the amount of teacher collaboration time using the lesson study model. The results of the present study will add to research on professional development as a means to enhance student achievement through teacher collaboration. The potential for a paradigm shift from a top-down method of professional development to teacher-directed professional development may change the way educators and administrators view teacher collaboration time.

Team: Michelle Adams

Question: What types of relationships and trends exist in the student interview mathematics assessments?

Abstract: In fall of 2006, every K–5 student who was enrolled at Paradise Professional Development School was given grade-level-specific mathematics pre-assessments through individual interviews that reflected conceptual understandings in number, from counting to place value. These qualitative assessments provide rich and meaningful data that allow teachers to make purposeful instructional decisions in their classrooms. The assessment responses not only assist the classroom teacher but are also converted into quantitative data that are used to report relationships, correlations, patterns, and trends in the students' conceptual understanding of number. My preliminary findings suggest that particular mathematics concepts have significant relationships and specific number concepts are grasped at a particular age or grade level. Post-assessments using the same mathematics assessments will be given to each student who participated in the fall mathematics interviews. The post-assessment interviews will be completed by June 2007, and the pre- and post-assessment data will be compared and analyzed, but will not be available at this time.

Team: Robbie Pearse

Question: How does the use of group positive reinforcement affect student behavior and academic performance for 8th grade students in the classroom?

Abstract: From December 2006 through May 2007, I studied the relationship between weekly positive reinforcement and behavior, and the relationship between monthly positive reinforcement and student performance in mathematics. Most 8th graders "have resigned themselves to the fact that classes are boring." We know that students must be engaged in learning to retain and apply it. Students were given the criteria they were expected to meet, and they were given models and examples that specified the expectations using the Responsibility Rubric.

Positive reinforcement is only positive reinforcement if it increases the likelihood that the behavior occurs. Behavior was based on teacher observation and referrals written last year as opposed to this year, with the introduction of several positive reinforcement techniques. Math achievement was based on quizzes, three chapter tests, daily classwork, and daily homework assignments. When the program was instituted, I reviewed the Responsibility Rubric with each class so that the expectations for classroom behavior and math achievement were clearly stated. The approach was to track points on a chart written on the dry-erase board in the front of the class. I was the only person who could deduct and give back points to the three teams in each of my five classes. Each class would receive one verbal warning at the beginning of the class; after that, the class understood that their points could be deducted without any further warnings. When I would approach the board where the points were being tracked, I would instantly get the students' attention, and the team would know exactly who to look at on the team for the point taken. The team would turn and tell the student what needed to occur so that they could gain the point back for the team. This approach took the pressure off me as being the "bad guy" or the "classroom cop." At the end of each week, the team with the highest points in each class (as long as all teams were above 7 points) would be rewarded with a "Choice Pass" coupon, an "IOU Quiz Point" coupon, or a "Homework Pass" coupon. Each member on the team would get to choose their reward. If they chose a "Choice Pass" it could be redeemed only on Friday for an item from the "Lame Prize Bucket" or could be redeemed at any time for school supplies they needed. The two most redeemed prizes were mechanical pencils and Jolly Ranchers. Math achievement was based on an overall classroom percentage so that no individual student could be singled out for their lack of performance. This also created a class against class competition. I would update the percentages each time my grade book was updated, so the students were aware on a regular basis how their class was doing against my other classes. At the end of each month, the class with the highest percentage would be rewarded with a class period of chosen activities from the "Jackpot Menu of Classroom Rewards." This study included 125 8th grade students in five Pre-Algebra 8 math classes at Robison Middle School, including 3 learning disabled students and 74 percent who spoke Spanish as a home language. The teacher has two years of teaching experience.

Team: Brent Bandhauer

Question: Do puppets, as a tool for teaching, improve student achievement?

Abstract: Beginning in January of 2007, I taught my careers education program to the 3rd and 4th grade students at two separate elementary schools. I divided the classes into a control group and an experimental group. My goal was to identify how much of an impact puppetry had on achievement. The control group received traditional approaches to teaching lessons such as storytelling, visual aids, and worksheets. The experimental group received the same instruction with the addition of puppetry incorporated into every lesson. At the conclusion of the five-week unit of study, the students were administered identical tests so I could compare the levels of achievement between the two groups. While the results didn't show a separation in achievement of the teaching approaches, all of the students showed strong understanding of the concepts taught. These results provide continued evidence that school counselors play a significant role in the education of students in public elementary schools.

Team: Dr. Sarah Munton and Jacqueline Brown

Question: Best Practices in Response to Intervention

Abstract: Charlotte Hill Elementary School is a pilot school for using Response to Intervention (RTI) procedures, and we are in our first year of implementation. RTI is a method in which the intensity of intervention increases based on individual student needs and how they have responded to previous intervention. The effect of using RTI is examined in regard to student and overall school achievement. Teachers and

Student Intervention Process (SIP) Team case managers are interviewed about the new procedures in order to make changes and improve the process. It is expected that this study will help us to learn the best ways to implement RTI procedures within our school. We were unable to measure the effect on overall school achievement at this time. The number of SIP referrals to special education remained the same as in the previous year. Changes in our school RTI procedures were made in midyear, and this appears to have made the process more manageable for teachers. We will continue to collect data in order to make improvements to our procedures.

Team: Josh Hager

Question: Will the implementation of a multiple intelligences–based project in a physics classroom at a performing arts high school lead to greater devotion to and understanding of the principles of physics?

Abstract: The use of multiple intelligences theory as a basis for curriculum design has grown since the theory's creation two decades ago (Gardner, 1983). Previously, educational theory and practice revolved around mathematical and verbal paradigms, ignoring learning potential in areas outside these two foundational ideas. Numerous studies conducted since the inception of multiple intelligences theory demonstrate that many students learn and retain knowledge and skills better when instructional emphasis promotes other intelligences than mathematical and linguistic. At a performing arts school, the use of various intelligences that are linked to their major areas of study may lead to greater motivation for students in the academic setting. At the Las Vegas Academy for International Studies, Visual and Performing Arts, there exists a disparity in student dedication between students' major classes and academic classes. Students spend a disproportionate amount of time focused on their classes of choice, often resulting in a lessening of effort in their academic classes. This motivation gap produces stress in a large percentage of students as they struggle to maintain grades in their academic classes. Observation and informal surveys of students at the Las Vegas Academy illustrate the frustration students experience in achieving balance between academic and major classes. In contrast to Clark County School District statistics, a large percentage of Las Vegas Academy graduates attend two- and four-year colleges. Postsecondary institutes evaluate applicant potential primarily through the success in and rigor of the student's academic classes; conversely, students audition for and attend Las Vegas Academy for more deeply studying performing arts subjects. The addition of this deeper pattern of performance study to a normal academic load theoretically creates a more rounded, stronger college applicant. However, the demand on student time and effort that is a function of this study duality often leads to lower student understanding and performance in academic classes. An additional drag on student achievement in academic classes is the enforced delineation between performance and academics. While tremendous opportunity exists for cross-curricular learning, actual manifestation of this opportunity occurs extremely rarely. Research in multiple intelligences theory (Gardner, 1993) illustrates that such cross-curricular learning benefits student achievement in a variety of classes, yet this knowledge is underutilized. Topics in art, music, dance, and theater can be seamlessly integrated with similar topics in social studies, English, science, and mathematics. Multiple and varied research supports this idea. Bridging this gap between these areas of study is crucial to the future success of Las Vegas Academy students. The arts are a lifelong pursuit, but the immediacy of high school and postsecondary educational needs must also be addressed. Utilizing a multiple intelligences approach to integrating these topics has been a successful model for curriculum design (Wright, 1997). Such an approach may be a solution to the educational gap that Las Vegas Academy students are experiencing. As a response to this problem, the question is posed: will the implementation of a multiple intelligences–based project in a physics classroom at a performing arts high school lead to greater devotion to and understanding of the principles of physics?

Team: Danielle L. Martwick

Question: Do graphic organizers increase student reading comprehension of informational text?

Abstract: From November 2006 through March 2007, I studied the relationship between the use of graphic organizers and student reading comprehension of informational text. In particular, I examined the use of a variety of graphic organizers and the use of a geography notebook. Reading comprehension of informational text was measured for this report using interim test results for 8th grade reading and world geography tests. In addition, I surveyed students to gain insights on their opinions of the use of graphic organizers while reading their geography textbook. I used a rubric to score the actual use of graphic organizers. My sample included 46 8th grade students. My preliminary findings suggest that graphic organizers, when used during the reading of informational text, are positively associated with improved reading comprehension. Student surveys suggest that the use of graphic organizers has improved their understanding of what they have read. I will be continuing to use graphic organizers through the end of the school year.

Team: Shari Ellis

Question: Do specialized tutoring and incentives improve high school proficiency scores and attendance in students with IEPs?

Abstract: From October 1, 2006, through April 1, 2007, we tracked attendance for all students with IEPs in grades 10, 11, and 12. In late January, a letter was sent to the parents of these students inviting them to a parent night where we described the program that we would be offering to help their children be successful on the proficiencies. We mailed 110 letters, and 22 parents attended. The parents and students were informed that each time students attended tutoring, their names would be put in a drawing for two iPod Nanos. The purpose of the incentives was to encourage attendance not only for tutoring, but overall daily attendance. The students were also given tickets each day they participated in the High School Proficiency Exams. With the financial help of UNLV Gear-Up, we offered a specialized after-school tutoring program taught by special education teachers in the areas of math and reading. To create enthusiasm for our project, we personally phoned parents of these students and explained how important the program was. Most parents thought it was a wonderful idea and assured us that their child would be attending. Tutoring started on February 5, 2007, and continued three days a week until the proficiency exams. Once the scores were in, the data were analyzed, with very disappointing results in both the areas of attendance and scores. During the research, new information came to light about the way we looked at the progress of this group of students and how we can use it to expand our research next year to more closely monitor and define what we consider progress.

Team: Cindy Kern
Question: Does an inquiry approach to evolution lead to conceptual change in my biology students?
Abstract: Every day students walk into a science classroom with preconceptions of science formed from their experiences. Science is often counterintuitive, making it difficult for students to learn and conceptually understand science understanding. The key to this action research is the development and implementation of an inquiry approach to evolution with a desired outcome of increased student achievement due to conceptual change. Data collection was analyzed for evidence showing each component of Posner and colleagues' model of conceptual change. The results indicate that inquiry leads to conceptual change.

Team: Eric Stensrud
Question: Action research on class Web sites
Abstract: It is often a familiar sight or even a rite of passage: the typical new teacher receives keys to his or her classroom and then begins to organize the pictures on the walls, the student seating arrangement, and even how their pencils will be placed in the drawer. A common ritual

after this organization occurs when all the experienced teachers periodically stop by to introduce themselves and leave boxes and file cabinet drawers labeled "favorite lessons." I remember when I received a plethora of materials from my coworkers and found it nearly impossible to decipher lesson plans. I was even more perplexed about how to amalgamate them into cohesive units. Many of the worksheets were a photocopy of a photocopy, and the idea of state standards was nowhere to be found. This past year, I relived this moment all over again. My wife began teaching this fall, and, as always, we organized her room and pencil drawer while teachers wandered into her room to say hello and drop off their file cabinets labeled "favorite lesson plans." The generosity of so many teachers was refreshing to watch, but someone needed to show them that the days of file cabinets and boxes were long gone and did little in helping teachers, new and experienced, to collaborate. For three years now, I have been using myteacherpages.com in order to construct and maintain a virtual classroom, which has allowed me to organize myself on the computer and which teachers, students, and parents can view. In 2005, I found myself wanting to become more organized for myself and my students. I began using www.myteacherpages.com to construct a virtual classroom where I can post notes and worksheets and maintain a calendar to which everyone has access. Many times I found myself sitting in a parent conference, and it was very clear that the parent had no idea when student work was due or when exams would be given. I went to work right away and started posting notes online, but as I continued to do this, I realized that in order to post a unit on the Internet, I needed to first sit down and figure out every worksheet, homework assignment, and the notes that I would use in class. But what was most important was the specific dates of when things were due and when the exam was going to be. By requiring myself to do all of these things, I became more organized than I could have imagined. Teachers would look at my Web site and comment that they found it easy to use and that they had used a worksheet or even an entire unit because it was very clear about what and how I was going to teach certain units. This

became the first step in teacher-to-teacher collaboration in which neither one had to physically sit down with the other in order to construct
common units.

Team: Michelle Barbee
Question: Reading strategies in transfer
Abstract: As a secondary English teacher for several years now, I have
come to know the meaning of functional illiteracy. This term is well
defined in Chris Tovani's *I Read It, but I Don't Get It*. Functional illiteracy can be spotted in students who can decode words in order to pro-
nounce them and may even be able to read aloud with unbelievable flair.
But ask those same students what they just read, and they have no idea
whatsoever. They have spent years evading the system, i.e., teachers'
questions, worksheets, and tests. They have become experts at finding
answers in a textbook for their fill-in-the-blank worksheets, experts at
regurgitating answers to tests because they heard the teacher talk about
it, and even experts at "word calling," which is reading aloud with absolutely no comprehension. All of these "tricks" enable students to get
through each school year unrecognized as practically illiterate.

Team: Ron Martini
Question: Does the use of classroom simulations increase student retention of information and their level of classroom engagement?
Abstract: From January 2, 2007, through May 4, 2007, I studied the
relationship between the use of classroom simulations and students' performance on specific curriculum power standards. Teachers in 3rd and
4th grade were given the opportunity to participate in facilitating classroom simulations for the purpose of providing students experiences that
promote the "doing" of learning. Student retention of information was
assessed through use of four assessment tools: (1) written exams,
(2) journals, (3) individual student interviews, and (4) skill-related performances. The different assessments were used to address individual

assessment style preference. Not all students were assessed at the conclusion of the simulations; instead, a random group of students was selected from each group. Postsimulation questions were asked of each student. Questions consisted of the following: (1) How do you best like to learn? and (2) What are some ideas you have for changes or improvements in the way you are taught? My initial findings suggest that students both retained more from instruction and preferred instruction where use of simulations was applied. Teacher interviews suggested that use of classroom simulations offered greater opportunity for real-world application of skills, retention of information, and active engagement of their students. Teacher participants agreed to continue use of classroom simulations for the remainder of this year and the next as a tool to increase student engagement and retention of curricular information.

Team: Kathleen Reiss

Question: Does teacher monitoring of agenda use improve homework turn-in rate for 7th grade science students?

Abstract: During February and March 2007, the relationship between teacher monitoring of agenda use and homework turn-in rate among 7th grade students in science classes was studied. Agenda-checking was done by a teacher in one room (Class T for "treatment" group) when homework was assigned, while in another classroom (Class N for "no treatment" group), the teacher prompted students to do homework and to log it in their agendas, but did not physically check that the agendas were completed. Compliance with filling out the agenda, the assignments, attendance, and homework completion was logged by the teacher in Class T on a class roster. The teacher in Class N daily logged the assignments, attendance, and homework completion on a class roster. Finally, the rate of homework turn-in for Class T and Class N was compared to see if there was a difference in homework turn-in rates. Cooperative special education classes were checked separately to ascertain differences in homework completion with and without treatment for this group.

Team: Ernie Rambo

Question: Does cursive handwriting instruction generate writing complexity?

Abstract: Over a 12-week period, 6th, 7th, and 8th grade students were provided with 10 minutes of daily handwriting instruction. Following each instructional period, students participated in their elective creative writing class, turning in a new piece of writing each week. Students were given pre- and post-tests to measure complexity of writing as well as tests to measure writing fluency. The pre-test and post-test prompts focused on different topics, but were designed to be of great interest to most students. Records of weekly assignments were maintained using the Nevada State Writing Proficiency Examination Analytic Scoring Guide for the idea trait to determine levels of complexity in writing samples. The scores of 8th grade students' Nevada Writing Proficiency assessments were compared with those of their peers who received no cursive handwriting instruction. All students participated in the cursive handwriting instruction, but were allowed to choose if they preferred writing in cursive or manuscript as they completed their assignments. Those who completed assignments in cursive received feedback on handwriting as well as a writing score. Although most students still prefer writing in manuscript rather than cursive, post-test scores generally showed an increase over students' pre-test scores.

Team: Nickole Backman and Amanda LaTurner

Question: Will drawing increase engagement and writing skill?

Abstract: From December 2006 to April 2007, we studied the relationship in the use of drawing first and then writing. From the drawings, we wondered how this process affected student writing within the 5th grade classroom of Amanda LaTurner. We began the project with 25 students and, with the loss of students for varying reasons, ended with 18 participants. We structured class rotations with 30-minute sessions, with all students taking a writing rotation. Four to five students with varying abilities were in each grouping. As the group director, I had a picture prompt with a definite problem within it and a series of seven questions related to the picture that were to be answered with a full sentence answer. They continued their writing by drawing three or more additional scenes. The students would draw the next scene and then write what was happening in the drawing. Data collection came from rubrics and student writing. Group time was evaluated at the end of each session with a rubric. After the completion of each story, the student and I evaluated the drawings and the completed story one-to-one. This was also with a rubric. Students made their own choices as to story prompts I had available and moved through the writing process at their own speed. Our preliminary findings indicate increased writing volume, more description within the story, and enhanced student enjoyment. We see that those students who followed the prompts as directed improved their story composition. We are unsure if the drawing/writing combination causes the improvement or if the small group routine is the catalyst.

Team: Brandy Johnson-Faith and Timothy Weekley
Question: Do inclusion and coteaching impact academic achievement for all students?
Abstract: Throughout the 2006–2007 school year, Brandy Johnson-Faith and Timothy Weekley studied the literacy growth of 3rd grade students learning in an inclusive classroom environment cotaught by a general education teacher (Johnson-Faith) and a special education teacher (Weekley). Specifically, we isolated three professional practices that in part define our inclusive setting: (1) employment of several models of coteaching; (2) facilitating homogeneous guided reading groups; and (3) designing differentiated literacy centers. Literacy mastery and growth were measured using a variety of assessments, including CCSD Grade 3 Trimester 1 Interim Reading Assessment, DIBELS (Reading Connected Text) Fluency Assessment, San Diego Quick Reading Assessment, and McLeod Assessment of Reading Comprehension. Our class is composed of 21 students, including 12 general education students and nine students with individualized education programs, or IEPs. Data

collection will continue through the end of the school year and will resume as this group of students moves into 4th grade. Our data currently suggests that inclusive coteaching is associated with a relatively high level of content mastery and an average to above-average rate of academic literacy growth for both general education and special education students.

Team: Maxine Davie

Question: Does action research positively change student attitude toward the usefulness of what they learn and their ability to effect change?

Abstract: From August to February of the 2006–2007 school year, our school was engaged in a large-scale service-learning project called the Silverado Empty Bowls Project in which several hundred ceramic bowls were created and decorated by students. These were then sold as part of a dinner where a simple meal of soup and bread was prepared and served by students. The bowls were kept by the guests as a reminder of all of the empty bowls in the world. Through the project, we raised over $7,000, which was donated to Friends in the Desert, an organization that feeds hungry people in Henderson. The basis for this effort were research studies that show the positive impact that teaching students to serve the community outside of the classroom has on student learning. Through the study, I was trying to determine answers to the following questions specifically: Can service learning positively affect student attitude about whether skills learned in school would be used in future life? Can service learning positively affect the opinion of art students as to whether their art-making skills could be used in future life? Can service learning positively affect the likelihood that students would think about community needs? Can service learning increase students' perceptions that they can personally impact their community? Can service learning increase students' impression that art has had an influence on society throughout history? Can service learning increase students' impression that art has an influence on society today?

Team: Linda R. Skroback-Heisler, EdD
Question: How do best practices from balanced literacy research affect ELL students' achievement in the Newcomer classroom?
Abstract: The purpose for this qualitative study was to explore the effect of best practices from the field of literacy used in one ELL Newcomer class in an elementary school. Twenty-seven 2nd to 5th graders attended the Newcomer classroom for three hours daily during one 14-week session (Part I) and one 11-week session (Part II). Research subquestions in Part I were modified in Part II to reflect students' changing needs. Data included teacher observations, field notes, attendance, daily notes, transcripts of oral language samples, running records, and student writing samples. In addition, two special subgroups were identified, and their progress was also tracked. Findings suggest that using a combination of best practices for 180 minutes daily resulted in the ELL Newcomer students' growth in language acquisition.

Team: Susannah Buckley, EdD
Question: Retention of high-efficacy, veteran teachers at Title I schools
Abstract: In one of the lesser-known provisions of the No Child Left Behind Act, a teacher-equity requirement orders states to ensure "poor and minority children are not taught at higher rates than other children by inexperienced, unqualified, or out-of-field teachers." This study set out to look at veteran, high-efficacy teachers who choose to teach at Title I schools in the CCSD. The study hoped to identify practices and school characteristics responsible for retention that could be replicated by other at-risk school sites. Commonalities in teacher survey responses, school improvement plans, and administration interview responses were analyzed. The proposed methodology was to perform a triangulation between the three data sources. Due to the qualitative nature of the responses, the process focused on themes and nuances in order to identify practices and school characteristics. Much of the research on teacher retention focuses on new teachers and their reasons for leaving the profession. Statistically, half of public school teachers leave the profession

within five years. Research on new teachers who stay in the profession has identified the following indicators as influencing their retention: strong support from the principal and fellow teachers, timely help with classroom management, and thoughtful mentoring in effective teaching techniques (*Education Week*, January 24, 2007). Other research findings reveal that the leading causes for teacher attrition are being assigned to classes that the teacher did not feel qualified to teach, not having a mentor during the first year of training, working conditions, and teachers not feeling that they are part of the decision-making process (*Finders and Keepers*, 2004; *Education Week*, November 15, 2006). Nearly three-quarters cited a lack of staff and principal support in their jobs, ever more challenging as classrooms become more diverse and demands for student achievement rise. The constant turnover in teaching vacancies costs taxpayers millions of dollars in the form of time lost to recruitment, monetary incentives, and monies paid for training. The monetary cost is inconsequential in comparison to the effect on student achievement. Teachers get better with time, but the high turnover leaves more classrooms run by novices.

Team: Linda R. Shillingstad

Question: Engagement in grades 9–12: A comparison of administrative/teacher perceptions

Abstract: A qualitative conceptualization of student engagement is presented based on a sampling of 10 classrooms at the Las Vegas Academy of International Studies. Using a Likert scale to gauge student engagement in both choice and required classes, administrators and teachers of those classes scored student engagement in individual and group work on a same-class, same-date basis. A sampling of 136 students in choice classes and 91 students in required classes compared administrator and teacher perceptions of the level of student engagement in each of the 10 classrooms. Samples 1, 2, 6, 8, 9, and 10 (136 students) are from choice classes and samples 3, 4, 5, and 7 (91 students) are from required classes.

A total of 227 students in a student population of 1,534 were sampled, a 6.75 percent sample of the total population. The students are members of a rigorous magnet high school program, grades 9–12, who choose a performing arts/international studies major and audition for entrance to the public school with requirements of a 2.0 GPA for entrance. They agree to maintain this GPA in all academic coursework, and the school enjoys a 96.3 percent daily attendance average and a 92.7 percent graduation rate. Seventy-five percent of the student population matriculates to a four-year university program. Administrators are given the task of determining student engagement as one of the tools used for teacher evaluation annually and quarterly, with little empirical evidence to support their decisions. The perception existed that teachers would be able to more accurately determine their students' engagement (cognitive, behavioral, and emotional) than administrators would, based on day-to-day student performance, work habits, proficiency on benchmarks provided by state and national standards, and quarterly assessments for each content area. Corroboration of administrative determinations was sought.

Team: Jim Cox

Question: The computer software program Supermemo and how it affects student test scores in science

Abstract: From November 2006 through April 2007, students were given access to a free computer program called Supermemo. This program is designed to increase memory retention after five study sessions. Students took chapter tests and semester exams without the use of the Supermemo program. Students were brought into the computer lab and given free access to Supermemo. They utilized the program for individualized study sessions. Those students who used the Supermemo program for at least 5 sessions showed an increase in test scores. Although all students were given the opportunity to use the Supermemo program, some chose not to. A survey was distributed to all students in an effort to find out the students' perception of their motivation for learning.

Team: Deb Trabert

Question: Do single-gender classes affect student achievement in writing performance?

Abstract: From September 2006 through April 2007, the relationship between single-gender classes and student performance in writing was studied. Student performance was measured for this report using five mock proficiency writing exams. In addition, the writing proficiency exam that was administered in 5th grade was also used for comparing writing achievement. The subjects were 104 of the students who took the proficiency writing exams in 5th grade in classes A, B, C, and D. The other students that were enrolled in the classes did not have a score from 5th grade or transferred in or out of the class during the school year. They were not included in the data used for reaching conclusions. Class A had 28 students of both genders (10 girls and 18 boys), class B had 28 students of both genders (9 girls and 19 boys), class C had 22 boys, and class D had 26 girls who were used in the collection of data. Gender-specific classes will continue through the end of the school year, and one more mock proficiency exam will be administered as a part of the semester final. It will not be a part of this study because the results are not available at this time. The author of this study concludes that single-sex classes can provide a positive and successful experience for girls. However, single-sex classes led to increased problems of behavior management and had little or no impact on raising the level of writing proficiency for boys.

Team: Amanda Bowen

Question: Can "coaching" eliminate reading symptoms so that students become better readers and their comprehension improves?

Abstract: From December 2006 through May 2007, I studied the effects of "coaching" on student performance in reading. Reading achievement was measured for this report using five tape-recorded reading assessments, three comprehension quizzes, and two Gates-MacGinitie tests (pre- and post-). I interviewed the student's reading teacher to see if any improvements in his performance were noticed in class. In addition, I surveyed both the student and the student's parents to gain their perspective on whether or not they noticed growth with his reading ability. At this time, data collection is still ongoing and will be available at a later time (June 21). However, my preliminary findings suggest that coaching on a regular basis is guiding the brain to correct the neural network so that the student is reading and comprehending better. The student's reading teacher indicated that she noticed improvement, especially with reading comprehension and his willingness to read in front of peers. The parents' survey suggested that they didn't notice a drastic change in his reading performance, but that homework seemed less frustrating for him and he was more willing to complete assignments. The student indicated that he feels more confident and that learning seems easier to him, especially in subjects that have always been difficult for him.

Team: Reta Troxell

Question: Does the use of a daily musical calendar spiral review improve math achievement in 1st grade students?

Abstract: The musical calendar spiral review was developed as a requirement for my master's degree in 1994. I have used the calendar since then to reinforce student skills. In the last three years I have seen a decrease in the number of teachers using a calendar to review and reinforce student math skills. From January 2007 through March 2007, I studied the relationship between the use of this calendar review and student performance in mathematics. The review was done 91 percent of the available school days. I stopped keeping track of student engagement after the first week because lack of engagement was not an issue. Any student who did not participate in one song always could be redirected to sing the next songs. No student was ever removed from calendar because of a behavior issue. Class A had been singing the review intermittently from September through December. Class B did not use a calendar review. Math achievement for this report was measured using a pre- and post-test of calendar skills and second interim math assessment results. My preliminary findings suggest that using the musical calendar spiral review, when implemented a high percentage of days and with high student engagement, is positively associated with student achievement in mathematics. Upon reflection, I find that while the review is associated with improvement in mathematics achievement, it was difficult to reserve 20 minutes daily. I am continuing the study through the end of the school year.

Team: Phyllis Tomlinson
Question: PreK study
Abstract: From January 2007 to April 2007, I studied the relationship between length of preK programming and student achievement. In this action research project, I tried to answer the following questions: Is there a difference in achievement between students who attend full-day versus half-day preK programs? Are there any differences in English language acquisition for students whose first language is something other than English between those who attend full-day versus half-day preK programs? I worked with two preK populations, a full-day and a half-day program. Both had a schoolwide Title I population, 80 percent English as a second language, and 100 percent eligible for free or reduced-price meals. I compiled data from the following: Brigance Test, LAS (Language Assessment Scales) scores, and Creative Curriculum Portfolio Assessment. I met with Jack Dailey and Gene Ward Elementary preK teachers and administration, coordinated LAS testing, and compiled and analyzed test results to determine which programming, half- or full-day, had the most impact on student achievement and English language acquisition. The findings from this action research project suggest that there is no significant correlation between more time in preK and better achievement on the LAS or the Brigance. Language acquisition scores, as measured by the LAS, were actually higher in the half-day preK program than the LAS scores in the full-day preK program. Even more interesting was the desegregation of four ELL students, who arrived after October 2006. For these students, the gains on the LAS were the highest growth scores.

Team: Lisa Tamura

Question: Does using a microphone and speakers improve students' phonemic/phonological awareness and grasp of phonics?

Abstract: For 11 weeks between December 2006 and mid-March 2007, my colleague and I studied the impact of using a microphone and speakers during a daily phonics/phonemic awareness drill in two 2nd grade classrooms. The daily 10-minute drill was designed around McCracken's book *Spelling Through Phonics*. Both classroom teachers agreed to follow a set of daily lesson procedures with their classes. Every week a different phonics focus skill was featured in the daily drill. The only theoretical difference between the classrooms is that in the treatment classroom, the teacher used a microphone and speakers to amplify her voice during the drill. In the control classroom, the same lesson was taught without the microphone and speakers. Students were assessed at the beginning of the project to determine baseline levels of phonemic/phonological awareness and phonics knowledge. We used the Qualitative Spelling Inventory (QSI) from Words Their Way to determine spelling level and grasp of phonics. For phonemic and phonological awareness, we used the Phonemic Awareness Assessment (PAA) from Rigby's *The Complete Phonemic Awareness Handbook*. Students were assessed weekly with a spelling test to determine grasp of the weekly focus skill. Students were given the QSI and PAA again at the end of the project to see what growth was made. Our findings suggest that although there are some limitations to our research design, there is enough of a positive relationship between the use of the microphone and students' increased grasp of phonics and phonemic/phonological awareness to warrant further study.

Team: Nicole Ralston

Question: Cameras in the classroom and their effects on student writing achievement

Abstract: From November 2006 to April 2007, I studied the relationship between the use of student-generated pictures and student performance in writing. Writing achievement was measured for this report using weekly writing assignments and trimester writing tests given grade-level-wide. The CCSD 6+1 Writing Traits rubric was used to assess these assignments with regard to ideas, organization, conventions, voice, word choice, and sentence fluency. The trait of presentation was not assessed. The 3rd grade class utilizing this method includes 18 students. Fifteen of these students speak Spanish at home and are ELL students. Two of these students have an IEP for reading and writing. Two of these students are in GATE. All 18 students and 100 percent of the school itself receive free lunch and breakfast. Data collection will continue through the end of the trimester using weekly writing assignments and the 3rd trimester writing test. This information is not available at this time. My preliminary findings suggest that student-generated pictures and cameras in the classroom, when used appropriately, are positively associated with improved student writing performance.

Team: Mary Sowder and Hillary Zeune deSoto
Question: Using science notebooks to build academic vocabulary for ELL students
Abstract: From January 2 to January 31, 2007, two teacher researchers studied the relationship between the use of science notebooks and the development of academic content vocabulary with a 3rd grade class of 18 students who were predominantly English language learners. Students' use of academic vocabulary was measured in open-ended pre- and post-tests, and assessed daily using a rubric to track the use of target content vocabulary in classroom discussions and in students' writing and drawing in science notebooks. Instructional practices designed to facilitate vocabulary development were analyzed by the teachers and evaluated for helpfulness by the students. The results of the study indicate that students did increase their use of academic vocabulary through the implementation of key instructional tools and strategies.

Team: Denise Roberts and Barbara Saling

Question: Does shared teaching contribute to improved spelling and reading development for 1st grade students?

Abstract: In this research project, two general education teachers (each with her own classroom) worked collaboratively with joint responsibility for student literacy achievement from September 2006 through May 2007. This collaboration allowed for more accurately leveled ability grouping and more frequent small-group instruction. In the process of the research, this scenario was termed "shared teaching." The purpose of this research project was to determine whether shared teaching positively impacted student spelling and reading development for 1st grade students.

Team: Catherine McCann

Question: Does recorder karate increase motivation to learn to read music and play the recorder?

Abstract: I was looking for something to motivate my students in 4th grade to practice their recorders on a regular basis so they would learn to read music from written notation. While doing research for the National Board for Professional Teaching Standards, I came across a concept called recorder karate. In the concept, students learn songs of increasing difficulty and earn "belts" (as in a karate class) for being able to pass off each of the benchmark songs. The belt songs increase in difficulty from white (easiest) to black (hardest). I was intrigued by the idea and wondered if I implemented the practice with my students whether I would see a greater gain in my students' ability to read music and play the recorder well. Achievement was measured using rubrics to score student ability to play music and read a musical score. Data collection began in late September and ended at the beginning of April. My findings suggest that there is a positive association between earning a belt for passing off songs and the motivation to continue practicing in order to learn another benchmark song and earn another belt.

Team: Jennifer Jenkins

Question: To what extent does phonemic awareness instruction affect 1st graders' reading performance?

Abstract: From September 2006 through April 2007, I studied the effectiveness of implementing daily phonemic awareness activities. I wanted to learn to what extent promoting daily phonemic awareness activities would enable students to improve their reading skills and thus improve their reading assessments and grades. My action plan included 15 minutes of direct phonemic awareness instruction each day. We began each lesson by reviewing letters and letter sounds. As I held a letter card, the students identified the letter and the sound the letter represented. We then completed various phonemic awareness activities that included identifying and changing beginning, medial, and ending sounds; breaking apart and putting together compound words; identifying and naming rhyming words; and chopping words and syllables apart. Each weekly lesson included the same skills throughout the week, but the activities varied each day of the week. Students' scores were analyzed on the following assessments: Qualitative Spelling Inventory, DIBELS, Developmental Reading Assessment, and trimester reading grades. The preliminary results were astounding. I discovered that not only did the students' reading scores and grades improve, but they also became more confident in their reading abilities and skills. The students were even transferring their newly gained knowledge from the phonemic awareness lessons into other reading and writing activities. I will continue the implementation of direct instruction of phonemic awareness activities and have encouraged my colleagues to do the same.

Team: Sarah Bryant and Laura King

Question: Does inclusion increase special education and general education students' achievement?

Abstract: From November 2006 through March 2007, I studied three classrooms that each had one special education student. These classrooms did a daily 15-minute review of the Power Standards to prepare for the IDMS test. In order to track growth, I looked at the students' results on the first and second trimester IDMS assessments. I also wanted to see if there was a difference between the inclusion and pullout classrooms in terms of IDMS results. Classroom 1 is the inclusion classroom with one of the special education students. Two of the students in this classroom are ELLs. Classroom 2 is a pullout classroom in which students receive all of their special education services in the resource room. This classroom has no ELL students. Classroom 3 is another pullout classroom. This classroom has two ELL students. The special education student did move halfway through the project. Data collection showed that all of the classes demonstrated overall growth on the IDMS test in reading and writing. The Power 15 standards group did not show as much growth on the IDMS test as the non–Power 15 standards group.

Team: Rebekka Balkwell and Kathy L. Batterman
Question: How do literature or trade books that demonstrate strong voice or word choice influence writing in 2nd grade students?
Abstract: From January 2007 through April 2007, I studied the relationship between using trade books to introduce voice or word choice writing traits and student performance in writing based on those traits. More specifically, I wanted to know if using trade books to teach the writing traits, which is a common practice, is truly beneficial and increases student performance. I chose to focus on word choice because in 2nd grade adjectives are a part of our language arts benchmarks and can sometimes prove to be challenging for students. I chose to also focus on voice because I wanted my students to showcase their individuality, humor, wit, and feeling when writing. I then used the Southwest Region Best Practices in Literacy handbook to find titles of books deemed appropriate to use to teach word choice and voice. I worked with my school's librarian aide to gather titles on hand and also checked books out from the Clark County Public Library. I focused on one trait for a week and used trade books that matched that trait to introduce the writing lesson each day. I switched between word choice and voice every other week.

The students started their writing piece with a brainstorm, and each day added more details, putting it into a paragraph form. Finally, the published paragraph was scored using the six-trait rubric on a 5-point scale. I recorded the score for the specific trait I was focusing on to chart student performance over time. Additionally, I began to score the actual trade book used in each lesson to determine if I felt it was a quality book that illustrated the trait well. The students also were able to vote "yes" or "no" on whether they believed the book showcased the trait well. I made a bulletin board titled "Rate the Trait," and each student had a card with his or her name and picture on it. They then placed their card on the "yes" or "no" side of the T-chart. We tallied votes and determined if the majority of the class believed the book I used was worthwhile. My preliminary findings suggest that using trade books to model word choice or voice does increase student performance over time.

Team: Tierney J. Cushman
Question: Vocabulary success
Abstract: From September 2006 through January 2007, I studied the relationship between vocabulary methodologies that would help students master vocabulary. At Fremont Middle School, 74 percent of students are second language students, with Spanish being the most common of first languages. Also, 81 percent of Fremont students are in the free or reduced-price meals program. Based on numerous studies, there appears to be a high correlation between poverty and language development. When English as a second language is added to this formula, vocabulary development is most crucial to academic success.

Team: Anne Harper and Rodney J. Lee
Question: A mark in time: A study on the impact of text-marking and reading strategies on student reading comprehension
Abstract: We wanted to know if the implementation of reading process (before, during, and after reading activities) coupled with text-marking strategies would improve student reading comprehension. We began our

journey to discovery in January 2007 and tracked our students' progress through April 2007. Text-marking was evaluated using techniques and a rubric developed by Scholastic Red. As well, student work was evaluated for implementation of the reading process as we moved through the unit. Students were also given pre- and post-surveys aimed at gathering information concerning attitudes about reading and strategies or techniques the students used to assist in their comprehension of text.

Team: Jenna Bruhn and Alison Carducci
Question: Does teaming improve students' academic achievement and address their affective needs?
Abstract: It was brought to our attention that our administration has seen a large achievement gap in students from 6th grade to 7th grade. It seems that for a large number of students who go on to the 7th grade, academic achievement decreases. As a result of this information, we implemented teaming as a solution. From January 2007 to May 2007, we studied the academic achievement among 7th grade students as well as their feelings toward school. We implemented a teaming strategy that allowed us to focus on a group of common students, both male and female, and grouped them according to identified challenges. We collected weekly observational data both on their performance in class and on affective goals set by us. We also compared their grades from first semester, before we used the teaming strategy, to second semester, when we collaboratively worked toward strengthening skills.

Team: Kathleen Sorrentino
Question: Do students with an IEP in an inclusion setting demonstrate rates of academic improvement similar to students without an IEP?
Abstract: From September 2006 through February 2007 we studied the relationship between the academic growth of students with IEPs in a general education setting and the growth rate of those students without IEPs. In particular, we examined the effect of an inclusive model of special education placement on achievement rates of students identified as

having a disability as compared to rate of improvement of students without a disability, whether degree of disability has an effect on rate of improvement, and whether growth rates can be established that assist in identification of which students require more intensive remediation. Achievement in reading, writing, and math was measured using curriculum-based measurement, IDMS scores, and, for 5th grade students, writing proficiency scores. Data collection will continue through the end of the semester using final IDMS, final benchmark Curriculum Based Measures (CBM) data, and state tests, information that is not available at this time. Our preliminary findings suggest that inclusion, even when implemented with consistent planning meetings that include discussion of key components, did not universally result in academic growth rates that match those of nondisabled peer performance when assessed using CBM. There was, however, at least one subject area at every grade level showing similar growth rates for the two populations. The students also appeared to benefit in terms of their mastery of grade-level curriculum standards as measured on the IDMS. Beginning skill level had a weak relationship on actual rates of progress in reading, with the exception of a moderate correlation found at the 5th grade level. Teacher interviews suggest that while coplanning improved quality of instruction, extra time was required by teachers to be able to fully discuss the key components and make the necessary preparations for differentiated lessons. Although a priority, other demands on teacher time had an impact on the regularity of these planning sessions. All participating teachers agreed to continue this study through the end of this school year and then conduct an additional evaluation.

Team: Sally Pettee

Question: School wellness policy impact action research project

Abstract: The purpose of this action research project was to determine whether or not the newly adopted Clark County School District school wellness policy had any effect, positive, negative, or no effect at all, on the students' perceptions of living a healthier lifestyle, the importance of exercise, and academic achievement. Research and a literature review were performed, and along with that information and the interpretation of the school wellness policy by the administration and staff of Eva Wolfe Elementary, several strategies were developed and implemented throughout the duration of the project. To help determine the level of impact, or lack thereof, data from the interim assessments, CRTs, physical fitness tests, and student-oriented surveys were gathered and analyzed. The conclusion of this project was that there was a positive effect, due to the fact that the students ate healthier and exercised more, and academic achievement results did not decrease.

Team: Kathy Steen

Question: Does the use of graphic organizers result in increased reading comprehension of the whole-class CORE reading program selections of Harcourt Trophies?

Abstract: This research project was a direct result of a districtwide mandate that each school use the accepted reading text or reading program daily for at least a 45-minute whole-class CORE reading lesson. For my intern and me, this meant grade-level instruction for our original class of 25 students who ranged from approximately 1.2 to 5.0 reading levels, with only four students at grade level. To assure these sessions would have the greatest benefit for all students and still use the program with integrity, we decided to supplement the program components to include at least one prereading, one during-reading, and one postreading graphic organizer, one of which gave an overview of basic story elements. Because one or more graphic organizers were already a strategy used by Trophies for each story, it was an easy task to adapt or occasionally add one more graphic organizer that fit our criteria. The hope was that graphic organizers would better focus and reinforce key words and phrases that would help all students, especially ELLs, remember story elements and therefore improve reading comprehension. Additionally, we hoped that focus on key words and phrases would improve end-of-the-selection test scores. Rubrics were used to evaluate one graphic organizer, the end-of-the-selection test, and teacher and student input for each story. Over the 10-week period, with 10 stories, the quality of the completed graphic organizers improved for most students, and test scores improved to varying degrees for the majority of students. Additional benefits were even more enlightening, including improved listening skills, improved oral discussions, increased knowledge of story elements for all students, and improved vocabulary development due to strategies used for graphic organizer instruction.

Team: Susan Sampson

Question: Does setting a words-per-minute reading goal really help improve reading skills such as fluency and comprehension?

Abstract: This project was designed to be a yearlong experiment. It began in October 2006 and will continue until the end of this school year. The results of this experiment reflect only the data that have been gathered from October 2006 to May 2007. I got the premise for this experiment when I first tested my students at the beginning of the school year. About three of my students had already met the end-of-the-year reading goal of 90 words per minute for 2nd grade. This brought up the question, "What am I to do with these students for the rest of the year?" Then I wondered, "How high could they go and still retain comprehension?" I decided to give them individualized reading goals of 45 words per minute higher than their baseline assessment, thinking that they *might* reach this "high" goal by the end of the school year. I told them that if a student met his or her set individualized goal, he or she would earn a prize. I went and bought a bunch of toys and put them in my cabinet under lock and key. I showed the toys off first and told them that they could earn a toy every time they met their reading fluency goal under my assessment. I needed to have something to compare my data to. I decided to compare my teaching strategy to the strategies of the other 2nd grade teachers at my school. With their cooperation, I learned how they went about teaching reading fluency, and they shared their students' DIBELS scores. Most of them had similar teaching strategies.

Although this information was not great to show contrasts, it was good in that it showed consistency over a larger test group—116 students compared to just 15 students in my class. In addition, I wanted an assessment that would check for comprehension. I chose to use the STAR assessment to measure this information. Gwen Marchand advised me to get the students' opinions. I thought it was a great idea and immediately made up pre- and post- student surveys that were administered to all of the 2nd grade students. While I gathered data, I decided to look at the information from different points of view such as boys versus girls, high versus low versus average growth scores, and ELL students versus primarily English-speaking students. Overall, setting fluency reading goals had a positive effect.

Team: Bonnie Darrell
Question: How does student choice of graphic organizers affect 6th grade writing achievement?
Abstract: Critical thinking skills are important in many areas of our lives and in school, especially in the science subject area. These skills are found in many content area standardized assessments, as well as in reading assessments, yet they are often weak skills for many students. After reviewing the state curricula standards, it seems that more difficult skills such as critical thinking and data interpretation are finding their way into all grade levels. Most of the scientifically based research that has been conducted has examined students' abilities to evaluate and read graphic representations of data. This research seeks to evaluate the students' abilities to choose and use graphic organizers to communicate their subject-matter understanding in their writing. Students need to be introduced to a skill such as using graphic organizers through a variety of teaching styles. Graphic organizers can help students achieve a greater understanding of material by reading, discussing, creating, and manipulating information, accommodating a wide range of learning styles. Modeling their use and teaching students to use and create graphic organizers on their own can be an effective teaching method that reaches many of

those different learning styles (Moore & Readence, 1984; Hall & Stangman, 2002). The Clark County School District has taken the need for middle school students to use higher-level thinking skills very seriously. Requiring students to regurgitate information on a multiple-choice test has not been shown to give students a lifelong love of science or a way to apply logical and critical-thinking skills. The entire middle school curriculum for the CCSD was rewritten, and new books were purchased for the 2006–2007 school year. Science teachers were offered multiple opportunities for professional development and training in the new "style" of teaching and student learning. Each teacher could then go back to his or her school and adapt the program to fit their style and the students' styles of learning. To help students organize their answers to the questions in the new Clark County School District Science 6 Curriculum, eight half-sheet graphic organizers were developed for students to choose from. Because every child learns differently, they also respond differently, and in turn, must be assessed differently on the questions given. From November 2006 to January 2007, the relationship between choice of graphic organizer and student achievement was studied. Two teachers participated in the study. They will be identified as Teacher A and Teacher B. Students using the new Science 6 curriculum are required to use a science notebook or science journal. All notebooks have a table of contents. Each lesson is numbered in the corner of their notebook paper. Students read in their text at home and answer their "In Question" in their notebook or journal and complete their vocabulary to prepare for the next day's lesson. Students then complete the lesson with the teacher. All procedures are written on the opposite page of the In Question and the vocabulary. Students are assessed on their knowledge and understanding of a lesson with an "Out Question," which is the last part of the lesson. As a prewriting technique, each teacher will break down the Out Questions into a manageable size so the students will be able to organize their thoughts and notes based on the information needed to answer the questions. Teacher A will give instruction on how to use the graphic organizers that are available to the students at the beginning of the unit. All Out Questions are written on a half-sheet of paper displayed on a counter, which allows students to go up and choose the ones that will best fit the answers they want to explain. Teacher A will compare students' results to Teacher B's results. Teacher B's students are not using graphic organizers for their Out Questions. Teacher B will be using blank half-sheets of paper only. Teacher A and Teacher B will use the same criteria to grade the Out Questions. During this process, Teacher A will be keeping a detailed journal of the project. Teacher A will keep student examples and take pictures of the criteria that will be used for grading the responses. Teacher A's instruction strategy is to have the different types of graphic organizers available on a table for students to choose to enable them to develop their thoughts and write their answers.

Team: Samuel Head

Question: Does inquiry-based learning enhance student achievement in core subjects?

Abstract: The relationship between the implementation of inquiry-based learning and student achievement in core subjects was studied over the period from November 2006 to February 2007. The research examined students' perceptions of how appropriate questioning could prompt critical thinking to construct personal meaning. Primarily, the research was gathered in one core subject—writing. An intermediate-grade departmentalized elementary writing classroom was the setting for the research. A random sample of 53 students was selected from four 5th grade classes. This grouping of students was categorized as Sample 1, with 26 students, and Sample 2, with 27 students. From that sample, a survey was conducted to determine baseline knowledge of the students' prior experience in inquiry-based learning. Writing skills were measured for this report using three writing samples and scores from the Nevada Writing Proficiency assessment. A rubric was used to score the writing samples. Achievement was measured by the students' general writing skills and their ability to generate and respond to probing questions. Of the students selected in the sample, 19 were Asian or Pacific Islander, 15 were White, 11 were Hispanic, and 8 were Black. Each of the participants spoke English fluently. The configuration of the core subjects, as well as the teachers of those subjects, changed prior to the end of the study. In the reconfiguration, the researcher, who was the language arts teacher, was reassigned to replace the mathematics teacher. However, data collection continued through the end of the study period. Based on the collected data, findings suggest that the continued use of this inquiry process at a high level will enhance student achievement, particularly in writing. Poststudy surveys of the students suggest that although achievement was enhanced through inquiry-based learning, the students appeared to be more engaged when writing persuasively. With the experience gained through the conduct of this study, the researcher will continue to implement inquiry-based learning when he is reassigned to the language arts classroom.

Team: Andrea Awerbach

Question: Whole-group instruction for students with autism

Abstract: This project has had quite an evolution. The report covers eight of the nine months of the 2006–2007 school year, beginning in August and ending in May. Initially, the team wanted to determine if students with autism would make academic and social progress if instruction focused on literacy and was provided via whole-group instruction. As is evidenced by the length and complexity of the previous sentence, this proved not to be an effective question. The research question and format were reworked several times. We took copious documentation notes and created and completed rubrics and informal assessments to obtain baselines. Still, the focus did not seem quite right. Different assessment tools were designed and implemented. It was suggested that the focus be narrowed to measure either social or academic growth. This did not seem an accurate picture of what was happening. Finally, it was the students and everyday events of the classroom that defined the project. Basically, we taught the way we thought it was important to teach and watched what happened. Rather than put perimeters or constraints on how to measure success, we looked at how the class and individual students had grown over the course of the project. There was significant growth for both staff and students. We might have missed this if we had been too narrow in our measures. Each year, our goal has been to improve the way our students interact with the world. This is important to us because we see autism as a disorder of isolation. We believe strongly in emphasizing communication and oral literacy above all else, and providing multiple opportunities for students to connect with adults, peers, and materials. As such, our instruction is provided in groups, both whole and small, and focuses on communication, oral literacy, social awareness, and self-help skills. Instructional levels and expectations are set at the level at which students can work either independently or with as little assistance as possible. There are multiple student choice sessions within a day, providing opportunities for students to extend their menus of preferred items while also learning to share materials and play with others. Our hope each year is that the class will become more student directed.

Team: Kaye Hartley

Question: Can a change in attitude from negative to positive increase a student's chance of improving academics, test scores, and behavior?

Abstract: This idea of whether or not teachers could get many students to change their attitudes from negative to positive and therefore become self-motivated had been nagging me for a long time. When Best Practice Research showed up on Interact one day in the fall of 2006, I decided it was now or never. So in October 2006, I outlined a program that I felt would help change students' negative attitudes to positive ones. I thought back to my own childhood and pondered what had made me have a positive attitude. From as far back as I could remember, which is probably 2 or 3 years old, the answer was my father and his knack for using famous quotations to capture my attention. For example, "Winners never quit, and quitters never win," "You can lead a horse to water but you can't make it drink," and "You can be anything you want to be if you want to bad enough" were a few of his quotations. He actually brainwashed my sister and me in a positive way. He was a college professor and basketball coach and often used quotations with his college students too. So I thought that maybe that would be a catchy way to get the attention of my students because quotes have rhythm and sometimes they even rhyme. Maybe that's why I had remembered quotes all those many years. In addition, I also recalled my first year teaching when I had two male students in my 5th grade class and they both had straight As. The two boys were best friends. I became curious about their backgrounds, so I studied their folders and found that one boy had only been in the United States for nine months. He was from Yugoslavia and spoke almost fluent English (little or no accent) that he had learned after coming to this country. He constantly talked about how he really appreciated being in this country. He talked about the other boy all the time, almost to the point of worshiping him. His IQ was listed as average, 105. The other boy was born in this country, and his IQ was 145. He was very meticulous and had beautiful handwriting. Finally, I concluded that the boy from Yugoslavia admired the other boy so much that he was inspired by him. Both boys, particularly the one from Yugoslavia, were self-motivated. Even though I was a new teacher, I was thinking about what makes students self-motivated.

Team: Mitch Johnson
Question: Does taking Cornell notes improve student understanding of physics as measured by the Force Concept Inventory Test?
Abstract: From August 2006 to June 2007, Cornell note taking was introduced to my honors physics and applied physics classes for a specific grade. Students were required to take notes with their personal whiteboards any time classmates were presenting to their class. The subjects were three classes of honors physics and two classes of applied physics at a stand-alone computer magnet high school. Preliminary results imply

that the way I implemented Cornell notes helped the honors students but didn't help or hinder their understanding. The 2007 results were taken at midyear, and, in comparison, the other results were at the end of the school year. Post-test results will be taken in June for final comparison. Next year I plan to incorporate more metacognition training with my students.

Appendix B

Action Research Proposal Form

The [Insert district or school name] is engaging in an exciting project to engage the intellect and discover the most effective professional practices of our teachers and administrators in a wide variety of areas. Individuals or teams (up to five people) may submit action research proposals on any topic, provided that the focus of the project includes student achievement and professional practices. All grade levels, all programs, and all subjects will be considered. The definition of "student achievement" may include state assessments but may also include district, school, and teacher-created assessments.

Instructions: Please copy and paste this form into the body of an e-mail (not an attachment) and submit the information electronically to the following address:
[Insert e-mail address]

You will receive an electronic confirmation of your submission within one school day. If you do not receive electronic confirmation of your submission, please call:
[Insert phone number]

The deadline for submissions is:
[Insert date]
We are unable to accept late submissions.

Part I. Contact Information

1. Primary Contact:

   Name:

   School or Department:

   Job Title:

   Primary Telephone Contact:

   Alternate Telephone Contact:

   E-mail Address:

   Mailing Address:

2. Additional Team Members

   Name:

   School or Department:

   Job Title:

   Primary Telephone Contact:

   Alternate Telephone Contact:

   E-mail Address:

   Mailing Address:

   Name:

   School or Department:

   Job Title:

   Primary Telephone Contact:

   Alternate Telephone Contact:

   E-mail Address:

   Mailing Address:

Name:

School or Department:

Job Title:

Primary Telephone Contact:

Alternate Telephone Contact:

E-mail Address:

Mailing Address:

Name:

School or Department:

Job Title:

Primary Telephone Contact:

Alternate Telephone Contact:

E-mail Address:

Mailing Address:

Part II. Research Questions

What question will your action research project consider? Please note that an effective research proposal must include specific references to student achievement and professional practices. We encourage creativity from a broad range of fields and grade levels. Following are some examples of interesting research questions:

- How does the use of homework menus affect math achievement for 7th grade students?
- How does the use of peer counseling affect student behavior, attendance, and academic performance for 9th grade students?

- How do prereading strategies influence reading comprehension for second-language alternative-school students?
- How does the use of peer editing affect writing performance for 5th grade students?
- How does integrated art and music instruction affect student understanding of advanced concepts in the fine arts?
- How does self-monitoring of rate, pace, and time influence student athletic performance?
- How does peer assessment affect work quality for career tech-prep students?
- How do environmental changes influence behavioral and academic performance of elementary special education students?

Part III. Student Population to Be Observed

Grade levels:

Special characteristics, if any:

Subjects:

Please note that the data you are gathering for this action research project are little different from the daily observations that teachers and leaders regularly make. Action research is distinguished by the consistent manner in which you make the observations and the perspective as teacher researcher. Accordingly, field notes can include typical classroom tools such as student portfolios, assessments, grade books, and other teacher notes. However, your final action research report *may not contain names or any other information identifying individual students. Photographs of students may be submitted only with written permission of parents.*

Part IV. Student Achievement
Data to Be Gathered

Please specify the assessments, observation instruments, or other specific student achievement data that are part of this project. State, school, or teacher-made assessments are acceptable. Researchers must have at least two observations for each student. The most effective research projects will have several measurements showing the relationship of the professional practices to student achievement over time.

Part V. Professional Practices to Be Observed

Please specify the professional practices that will be observed. These are adult actions—specific and observable behaviors of teachers, administrators, or other adults who are the subject of the research project. The most effective research projects will record a range of professional practices. For example, rather than an observation that "the teacher used differentiated instruction," a more effective approach would be to specify the precise differentiated instruction strategy that was used and also record, using a scoring rubric, the degree of effectiveness of that strategy on a scale of 1 to 4.

Part VI. Support, Permission,
or Resources Required

Most action research projects are undertaken in the regular course of the duties of the teacher researcher, and therefore no special support, permission, or extra resources are required. If that is the case for your proposal, please simply say "None" in response to this section. However, if your project will require any support (financial, administrative, manpower, physical space, equipment), permission (administrative, parent, etc.), or resources, please specify those needs here. ***Please specify how your project team will secure the necessary support, permission, and resources to complete your project.***

APPENDIX C

SCORING RUBRIC FOR ACTION RESEARCH PROPOSALS

Total Score: _____

Proposal Number: _____

Primary Contact Name: _____

A. Research Question SCORE: ___	4. Question has vital importance and clear relevance to district needs.	3. Interesting question, clearly relevant to district needs.	2. Question already addressed by significant body of research.	1. Question unlikely to reveal new or relevant insights.
B. Student Data SCORE: ___	4. Data sources are related to research question and meet high standards of validity and reliability.	3. Data sources are related to research question and have adequate validity and reliability.	2. Data sources somewhat related to research question, and validity and reliability are uncertain.	1. Data sources have limited relationship to research question and are unlikely to yield valid and reliable observations.
C. Professional Practice Data SCORE: ___	4. Professional practice observations are related to research question, are clear and systematic, and represent a range of performance.	3. Professional practice observations are related to research question and are clear and systematic.	2. Professional practice observations are somewhat related to research questions and have limited clarity.	3. Professional practice observations have limited relevance to research question and are unsystematic.

D. Resource Requirements SCORE: ___	4. Proposal either requires no additional resources or clearly provides for all resources, support, and permission.			1. Proposal requires resources, support, or permissions that are not provided in the proposal.
TOTAL: _____				

Appendix D

Sample Action Research Proposal

E-mail to
[Insert e-mail address]

Part I. Contact Information

1. Primary Contact

    Name:
    School or Department:
    Job Title:
    Primary Telephone Contact:
    Alternate Telephone Contact:
    E-mail Address:
    Mailing Address:

2. Additional Team Members

    Name:
    School or Department:
    Job Title:
    Primary Telephone Contact:
    Alternate Telephone Contact:
    E-mail Address:
    Mailing Address:

Part II. Research Questions

*   How do math journals influence student achievement in grades 9 and 10 mathematics?
*   How do home language math journals influence student achievement in grades 9 and 10 mathematics?

- What are the advantages and disadvantages of home language math journals, rather than English language math journals, for students, teachers, and parents?
- What are the advantages and disadvantages of math journals for learning disabled students?

Part III. Student Population to Be Observed

Grade levels: 9 and 10
Special characteristics, if any: 40 percent of these students have a primary language other than English; 12 percent are learning disabled.
Subjects: Mathematics

Part IV. Student Achievement Data to Be Gathered

- Weekly quizzes (teacher-created)
- District standards-based tests (IDMS assessments)
- Chapter tests (textbook)
- Final exam results (math department)
- Semester grades (teacher-assigned)
- Rubric-based score on math journals (new rubric I have created in collaboration with ESL teacher)

Part V. Professional Practices to Be Observed

- Support for creating math journals—The math and cooperating ESL teacher will assist students as they create math journals and apply the information. We will include exemplary models of math journals, have students practice scoring anonymous student work in math journals, and allow each student to choose to use English or his or her home language. After this instruction, students will provide anonymous feedback to the teachers, assessing the clarity of the instruction and student interest in the journal project.

• Teacher feedback—Teacher feedback will be evaluated quantitatively in terms of the number of questions posted by the teacher in the math journals and the number of productive questions—those that elicited a response from students in subsequent journal entries.

• Use of math journals—The project will evaluate the frequency of journal entries once weekly for the 20 weeks of this research project. Scoring totals in this category will be from 0 to a maximum of 20 for the project period.

• Quality of math journals—The project will evaluate the quality of journals using a 4-point rubric.

> 4 = Entries are directly related to the math work for the week and include multiple insights on student learning, along with specific steps the student has taken for improved performance.
>
> 3 = Entries are related to the math work for the week and include at least one insight on student learning.
>
> 2 = Entries are somewhat related to the math work and contain minimal insights on student learning.
>
> 1 = Entries are unrelated to math and disconnected from student learning.
>
> 0 = No journal entry

• Student language—Each journal will be coded based on the language chosen by the student for the journal entries.

• Student special needs—Each journal will be coded with student special needs.

Part VI. Support, Permission, or Resources Required

None. The math department chair and school administration are aware of my intention to use math journals, including home language journals, and have no objection to this project.

SAMPLE ACTION RESEARCH REPORT

Do Home Language Math Journals Improve Math Achievement in High School?

Abstract

From December 2006 through February 2007, we studied the relationship between the use of math journals and student performance in mathematics. In particular, we examined the use of English journals and home language journals (Spanish). Math achievement was measured for this report using four quizzes and two chapter tests. In addition, we interviewed participating teachers to gain insights on the advantages and disadvantages of their use of math journals. Finally, we used a rubric to score the actual use of the math journals in each participating class. Class A included 10 students who spoke English as their primary language and 16 students who spoke Spanish at home. Class B included 11 students who spoke English as their primary language and 10 students who spoke Spanish at home. Data collection will continue through the end of the semester using final exams and state tests, information that is not available at this time. Our preliminary findings suggest that math journals, when used at a high level, are positively associated with improved student performance. Teacher interviews suggest that although math journals improved student understanding and saved teachers time in remediation, extra time was required by teachers to provide meaningful review and feedback to students. All participating teachers agreed to continue this study through the end of this school year and then conduct an additional evaluation.

Sample

This study included 9th grade students in two math classes at Jefferson High School, including 10 learning disabled students, 3 of whom spoke Spanish as a home language. The teacher for Class A had 17 years of teaching experience and a master's degree. The teacher in Class B had 15 years of experience and a master's degree. The cooperating ESL teacher for both classes had seven years of experience and a master's degree.

Reflections and Lessons Learned

Our research project could have been improved in three ways. First, we should have pre-tested the math journal rubric to make it more specific and user-friendly. Second, we should have provided more familiarity and professional development on the use of the math journal before starting the study and using it with real students. Third, we should have solicited narrative feedback from students about their experiences with the math journals.

Future Research

We intend to continue this research with additional assessments, including final examinations and state exams. We also intend to create a "Version 2.0" of the rubric and provide more explicit adaptations for special education and second-language students. We also intend to extend the use of math journals into advanced classes for the next school year.

Findings

Math journals, when implemented at a high level, are positively associated with improvements in student achievement. Figure E.1 (see p. 160) shows student performance on four quizzes, in which students could score from 0 through 10 (missing students were not counted in the averages). Although the classes had similar achievement on Quiz 1 scores, Class A made more progress on subsequent quizzes. Each class had five learning-disabled students, and Class A had a higher proportion of students who spoke Spanish at home. The two classes had teachers with similar experience, degrees, and professional backgrounds.

Figure E.1

Average Quiz Scores

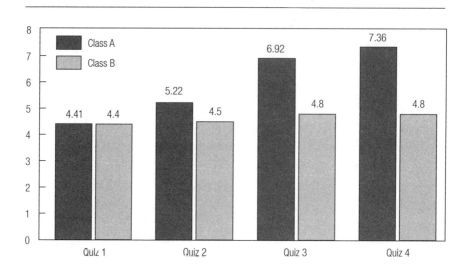

A review of the math journals, however, revealed a significant difference in the two classes' scores, as shown in Figure E.2. Each student math journal was scored using the following rubric:

4 = Entries are directly related to the math work for the week and include multiple insights on student learning, along with specific steps the student has taken for improved performance.

3 = Entries are related to the math work for the week and include at least one insight on student learning.

2 = Entries are somewhat related to the math work and contain minimal insights on student learning.

1 = Entries are unrelated to math and disconnected to student learning.

0 = No journal entry.

Figure E.2

Average Rubric Scores on Implementation of Math Journals

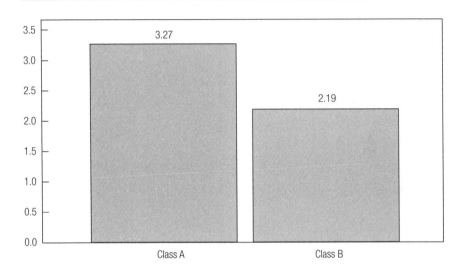

Spanish-speaking and English-speaking students had identical average rubric scores in Class B (2.2). In Class A, however, English-speaking students had slightly higher rubric scores for their math journals (3.5) compared with their Spanish-speaking colleagues (3.1).

Perhaps the most striking finding is the change in the classes' performance between two chapter tests (see Figure E.3, p. 162). Class B test performance actually dropped, yet Class A showed significant improvement. The conclusion for Class B is not necessarily that the use of math journals hurt academic achievement—certainly Class B experienced very modest gains in quiz performance. Rather, the inference should be that when implementing math rubrics, only the highest levels of implementation (3 or 4) are associated with improvements in achievement. It also appears that the high-level use of Spanish-language math journals does not hurt student performance, even though it does take time away from students' and teachers' direct focus on math problems.

Figure E.3

Changes in Chapter Test Scores

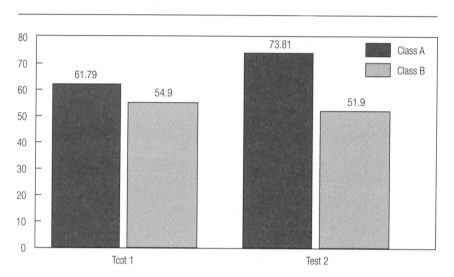

Conclusions

In the following section, we have outlined our findings as they relate to the study research questions:

- *How do math journals influence student achievement in grades 9 and 10 mathematics?* It appears that math journals are associated with higher achievement in grade 9 math only when journals are implemented at the highest levels on our four-point rubric.
- *How do home language math journals influence student achievement in grades 9 and 10 mathematics?* It appears that the use of home language does not hurt student achievement, and it may be associated with improved achievement. But whether the cause of improved performance for Group A was the use of home language or the use of the math journal is a subject for further study.
- *What are the advantages and disadvantages of home language math journals, rather than English language math journals, for students, teachers,*

and parents? What are the advantages and disadvantages of math journals for learning disabled students? The primary disadvantage of home language math journals was the extra time required for students to complete them and for teachers to provide feedback. However, the rubric provided a quick and efficient way to provide frequent feedback to students and to evaluate the journals. The 10 learning disabled students in the study completed math journals without any notable accommodations. As with all assignments, learning disabled students were given extra time to complete them, and some students chose to use word processors rather than pen and paper for their journals.

Suggestions for Future Research

We will continue this study, gathering student data from final exams and state exams. In addition, we will expand this study to include other classes that use no math journals at all or classes that are using math journals in a different scope or intensity from how classes used them in this study. We would also like to explore different methods of math journals, including the use of colors, three-dimensional objects, and computer graphics in math journals. Finally, we plan to explore early next year the use of math journals for pre-assessment in order to identify student needs from the earliest days of class and thereby create differentiated instructional plans for our students.

Contact Information
1. Primary Contact:

Name:
School or Department:
Job Title:
Primary Telephone Contact:
Alternate Telephone Contact:
E-mail Address:
Mailing Address:

2. Additional Team Members

    Name:

    School or Department:

    Job Title:

    Primary Telephone Contact:

    Alternate Telephone Contact:

    E-mail Address:

    Mailing Address:

RESEARCH PROJECT REVIEW FORMS

Please save this form and other notes as part of your action research records to be submitted with your final project report. Thanks!

Research Checklist

[Insert district or school name]

Action Research Seminar
[Insert date]

Instructions: This checklist will help you get the most out of this seminar by helping you to review your proposal and plans in a systematic manner. As with each part of the seminar, we'll use a "red/yellow/green" system to provide individualized help. If you are working well on your own, please display your green card. If you have a question, please display the yellow card. If you are stuck and need immediate assistance, please display the red card.

Action Research Component	Complete?	If Not Complete, I Need the Following
1. Research questions		
2. Student achievement indicators—the specific tests, quizzes, rubrics, observation instruments, questionnaires, or other assessments you will use		

Action Research Component	Complete?	If Not Complete, I Need the Following
3. Teacher-leader indicators—the specific questionnaires, observation instruments, rubrics, or other assessments you will use		

4. Adaptations and accommodations for
  a. Special education
  b. English language learners
  c. Other special needs		

5. Data collection plan—a written description of how you will collect data		
6. Analysis plan—a written description of how you will analyze the data to answer your research questions		

Student Assessment Review

[Insert district or school name]

Action Research Seminar
[Insert date]

Instructions: Please use this table to review your plans for student assessments in your research. The goal is not the creation of perfect assessments, but rather the continuous process of professional reflection by comparing assessment practices to a set of criteria. You can then use that reflection to improve classroom assessment.

Student Assessment Instrument (Please identify the test, quiz, rubric, or other assessment instrument.)	**Validity**—Are we testing what we think we are testing? (Think of a math test in English given to ELL students—are we testing math or English?)	**Reliability**—Are the results consistent? (Think of a scale—each time you weigh a pound of bananas, it should show "16 ounces.")
1.		
Improvements for Instrument #1:		

2.		
Improvements for Instrument #2:		
3.		
Improvements for Instrument #3:		

Teaching and Leadership Practice Review

[Insert district or school name]

Action Research Seminar
[Insert date]

Instructions: Please use this table to review your assessment of teaching and leadership practices. This is almost always the most challenging part of any research project, as professional and leadership practices are notoriously difficult to observe in a systematic manner. That is why this activity is essential—effective researchers are always improving their observation methods.

Teaching/ Leadership Observation Instrument (Please list observation instrument here.)	Clarity and Consistency (Share your instrument with a colleague and let him or her ask clarifying questions.)	Continuum of Observations (Does the instrument provide for a continuum of at least four levels of observation?)	Specificity (How can the instrument be made more specific? If you were being observed, how could you make it more fair and objective?)
1.			

Modifications to Instrument #1:			
2.			
Modifications to Instrument #2:			

Data Collection and Analysis Review

[Insert district or school name]

Action Research Seminar
[Insert date]

Instructions: Please use this form to review and, if necessary, improve your plan for data collection and analysis. These open-ended questions are designed to help you consider unexpected events and anticipate typical challenges in action research.

1. Missing Data: What will I do if students are absent for some of the assessments or they are absent when I am providing the teaching practices I want to evaluate?

| |
| |
| |
| |
| |

2. Midcourse Corrections: What will I do if I discover that I've made a mistake in my instruction, curriculum, or assessment?

| |
| |
| |
| |
| |

3. Data Displays: How will I display my data—graphs, charts, tables?

4. Data Gathering: How will I gather and record data? Will this give me the data I need to produce the data displays I described in question 3?

Please write a hypothesis—what you think will happen as a result of your project. Hypotheses are typically "If . . . then" statements. For example, "If my students write math journals in their home language, then their proficiency in the open-response questions in math problem solving, with English responses, will improve."

For my action research, one of my hypotheses is:

What would a graph of your results look like if your hypothesis is supported by your data? Please draw a sample graph in the space below.

What would a graph of your results look like if your hypothesis is not supported by your data? Please draw a sample graph in the space below.

APPENDIX G

SAMPLE PARTICIPANT REPORT

Do Graphic Organizers Increase Student Reading Comprehension of Informational Text?

Abstract

From November 2006 through March 2007, I studied the relationship between the use of graphic organizers and student reading comprehension of informational text. In particular, I examined the use of various graphic organizers and a geography notebook. For this report, I measured reading comprehension of informational text using interim test results for 8th grade reading and world geography tests. In addition, I surveyed students to gather their opinions on using graphic organizers while reading their geography textbooks so that I could gain insight into their views. I used a rubric to score the actual use of graphic organizers. My sample included 46 students in 8th grade. My preliminary findings suggest that the use of graphic organizers while reading informational text is positively associated with improved reading comprehension. Student surveys suggest that the use of graphic organizers improved their understanding of what they read. I will be continuing to use graphic organizers through the end of the school year.

Sample

This study included 46 students in 8th grade at Jerome D. Mack Middle School. English language learners accounted for 33 percent of the students, and 13 percent were learning disabled students. I, the teacher, had six years of teaching experience and a master's degree.

Findings

Graphic organizers, when implemented at a high level, are positively associated with improvements in student achievement. The chart in Figure G.1 shows student performance on five tests. Possible student

Figure G.1

Test Performance

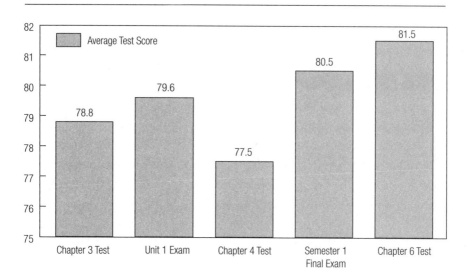

scores were 0 percent to 100 percent (missing students were not counted in the averages).

The use of graphic organizers was implemented beginning in early November 2006. The Chapter 3 test was given on November 10, 2006, less than two weeks after implementing the use of graphic organizers. The students were very receptive to a change in learning style. Positive test results followed, with students averaging 78.8 percent on the exam. Five students did not take the exam. The Unit 1 exam was given on November 22, 2006. This test reviewed concepts that students had previously learned. The class used graphic organizers in the review for the unit test. Students reviewed each chapter by creating graphic organizers to help them categorize the information they were reviewing. Students performed well on the Unit 1 exam, scoring an average of 79.6 percent. Three students did not take the test due to frequent absences. The Chapter 4 test is the abnormality in the steady increase of test scores. The Chapter 4 test was administered on January 9, 2007. One possible explanation for the decrease in test scores was my absence during three days of instruction on this chapter. I did not plan to have the students complete graphic organizers in my absence; rather, they completed worksheets that accompany the textbook. Another possible explanation is that students had just returned from the winter vacation and may not have been prepared to resume their studies. Both the Semester 1 final exam, administered on January 19, 2007, and the Chapter 6 test, administered on February 14, 2007, continued to show an increase in test scores.

Interim reading assessment scores (see Figure G.2) were used as a tool to determine growth in student comprehension. I administered the first-quarter (Q1) reading interim test on November 1, 2006. At about the same time, students began using graphic organizers; therefore, the Q1 interim test served as a pre-test for the students. I administered the second-quarter (Q2) reading interim test on February 1, 2007, after

Figure G.2

8th Grade Reading Interim Test Scores

Number of Students

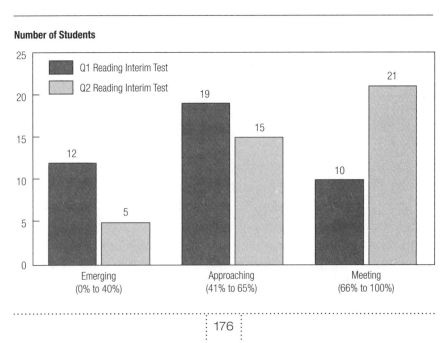

| | Emerging (0% to 40%) | Approaching (41% to 65%) | Meeting (66% to 100%) |

three months of graphic organizer use in the world geography class. Scores increased dramatically between the Q1 and Q2 reading interim tests. The number of students who scored between 66 percent and 100 percent more than doubled, with 21 of the students meeting or exceeding the standard for the Q2 interim test. The number of students in the emerging category—with scores of 0 percent to 40 percent—was cut by more than half. The increase in students meeting the standard contributed to the decrease in students approaching the standard.

In addition to the use of graphic organizers, these results can be attributed to the English teacher for her determined teaching and use of cross-curricular instruction. The results also provide insight into students' possible scores on the Criterion-Referenced Test, but those results have not yet arrived.

The number of students who performed well on classroom tests was very high. Approximately 70 percent of the students scored 70 percent or

Figure G.3

Test Score Percentages

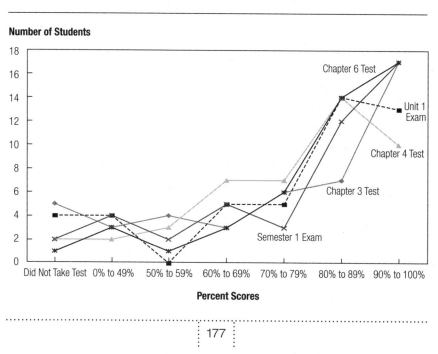

higher on the tests. About 60 percent of the students scored 80 percent or higher, and 32 percent of the students scored 90 percent or higher.

To measure how well students used the strategy, I scored each graphic organizer using the following rubric:

4 = The graphic organizer was complete and accurate. Additional information was provided that went above and beyond the requirement.

3 = The graphic organizer was complete. Most of the information in the organizer was accurate.

2 = The graphic organizer was partially completed. Some of the information was accurate.

1 = The graphic organizer was incomplete.

0 = The student made no attempt to complete the graphic organizer.

The rubric scores shown on the chart in Figure G.4 are the average student scores on the graphic organizers. The average rubric score for the Chapter 3 test (3.20) was slightly higher than the score of the Unit 1 exam (3.11). This could be attributed to students' excitement at beginning a new way of learning. The students were engaged in learning and displayed on-task behaviors throughout the implementation of graphic organizers. The rubric score for the Chapter 4 test (2.6) is expected. Only one rubric was used during this chapter. The students returned to the mind-set of completing worksheets. When a graphic organizer was used during the whole research period, 20 percent of the students failed to complete the assignment. By the end of the research period, students had become quite proficient at completing the graphic organizers in a way that would impact their learning.

To measure use of the geography notebooks as a strategy, I scored each student notebook using the following rubric:

4 = The notebook had all of the required elements. The information was accurate.

Figure G.4

Rubric Scores on Use of Graphic Organizers

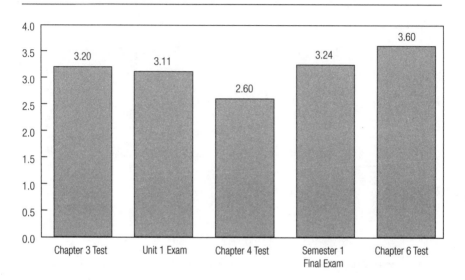

3 = The notebook was complete. Most of the information was accurate.

2 = The notebook was partially completed. Some of the information was accurate.

1 = The notebook was incomplete. It will have no influence on student performance.

0 = No notebook submitted for scoring.

Average rubric scores for the notebooks for specific chapters are shown in Figure G.5 (see p. 180).

I surveyed the students to gather their opinions about using graphic organizers while reading their geography texts. Students were asked to choose one of the following:

• The use of graphic organizers had a positive impact on my comprehension of the information I read in my geography textbook.

Figure G.5

Rubric Scores on Geography Notebooks

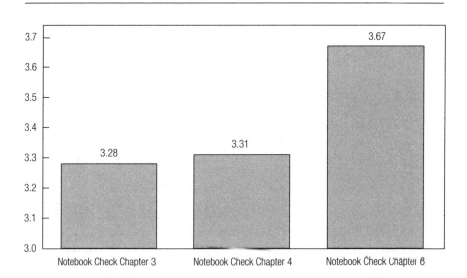

• The use of graphic organizers had no impact on my comprehension of the information I read in my geography textbook.

The results of the survey (shown in Figure G.6) indicate that 82 percent of the students believed that using graphic organizers had a positive impact on their textbook comprehension.

I also surveyed the students about their opinions on using geography notebooks for recording vocabulary and information about landforms and locations. Students were asked to choose one of the following:

• The use of a geography notebook had a positive impact on my comprehension of the information I read in my geography textbook.

• The use of a geography notebook had no impact on my comprehension of the information I read in my geography textbook.

At the beginning of each period, the students wrote information in their geography notebooks. This was an individual warm-up activity.

Figure G.6

Student Perception of the Use of Graphic Organizers

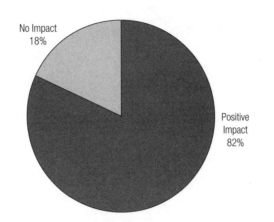

My expectation was that students would enter the room and begin recording information in their notebooks. This information included vocabulary and definitions that the students needed to locate in their textbooks without using the glossary. They also noted any pertinent landforms or locations that were covered that day. The results of the survey indicate that only 66 percent of the students felt that using geography notebooks had a positive impact on their textbook comprehension (see Figure G.7, p. 182).

Conclusions

In the following section, I outline my findings as they relate to the study research questions:

- *How can graphic organizers be used to check for understanding during reading?* It appears that the graphic organizers helped students categorize what they were reading. Students completed the graphic organizers while they read the textbook. The graphic organizers also led to more classroom discussions about what students were reading. When a student shared information from a graphic organizer, other students

Figure G.7

Student Perception of the Use of Geography Notebooks

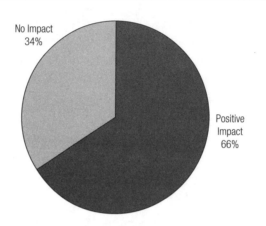

No Impact
34%

Positive
Impact
66%

often gained information that they might not have put in their own organizers. Overall, the increase in classroom discussion surrounding the organizer showed me that students comprehended what they were reading.

- *How does the utilization of graphic organizers for formative assessment increase student comprehension?* It appears that graphic organizers are associated with higher achievement in reading informational text. The use of graphic organizers for formative assessments increased student knowledge and prepared students for the summative tests. Student test scores increased during the period when they used graphic organizers. In addition, the students believed that graphic organizers positively affected their learning.

- *How does the use of a geography notebook increase student achievement?* It appears that the use of a geography notebook does not significantly increase student achievement. I believe that it is important for students to learn geographical vocabulary and locations; however, there may be a more effective strategy.

Reflections and Lessons Learned

Through observations and self-reflection, I found two themes to focus on in improving my future research. First, my research project could have been improved by offering a pre-test and post-test to the students. I did use the interim exam as a pre-test and post-test, but I would like to offer a test that is specifically related to geography. Second, I would not include the use of geography notebooks in further research. I don't feel that they improved student achievement.

Suggestions for Future Research

I will continue this study throughout the year. I would like to gather data from final exams and the Criterion-Referenced Test. In addition, as the social studies department chair, I would like to extend the use of graphic organizers throughout the department. I would like to have open dialogue with my peers during structured teacher planning time about the effectiveness of graphic organizers. I want to reach more students. Finally, I intend to modify the use of geography notebooks so that they positively affect achievement rather than serving as a filler activity.

Contact Information
Primary Contact
Name: Danielle L. Martwick
School: Jerome D. Mack Middle School
Job Title: 8th Grade World Geography Teacher
Primary Telephone Contact: 702-799-2005
Alternate Telephone Contact: 702-234-4445
E-mail Address: dlmartwick@interact.ccsd.net
Mailing Address: 5892 Wildhorse Ledge Ave., Las Vegas, NV 89131

Source: Adapted with permission from Danielle L. Martwick.

Appendix H

Guidelines for Data Walls, or "The Science Fair for Grown-Ups"

By Douglas B. Reeves, PhD
The Leadership and Learning Center
www.LeadandLearn.com
(866) 399-6019

One of the most powerful techniques that educators and school leaders can use to improve decision making in the classroom, school, and district is the "Data Wall." Ideally, the Data Wall is a portable display, using the cardboard three-panel display frequently used for student science fairs. When administrators gather to discuss their ideas for improving student achievement, Data Walls provide a rich source of information about the strategies employed in each school. Within each school, Data Walls can be the focal point for faculty discussions on improving student achievement. For principals and teachers who are already using data to guide instructional decision making, the use of a Data Wall will not create any additional work. For leaders who are not using data to guide their decisions, Data Walls provide a valuable technique to jump-start their work. Most important, this technique will ensure that the analysis of student data is not isolated to a single seminar or a staff development program on data, but rather becomes a continuous part of faculty and administrative decision making throughout the school year.

Three Essential Parts of the Data Wall:
1. External data, such as state test scores.
2. Internal data (classroom assessments or other school measurements involving teaching practices chosen by the school that reflect its unique needs).
3. Inferences and conclusions (drawn from the data).

Information for the Panels:

Left Panel: Includes tables, charts, and graphs that illustrate state test scores for the school and district. There may also be narrative comments, such as, "84 percent of our students are proficient or higher in mathematics according to the state test scores, and 78 percent are proficient according to a district test. A review of the last three years of data shows consistent progress on both state and district measurements, with particular gains in the problem-solving portion of the math assessments."

Middle Panel: Includes data on teaching strategies associated with mathematics followed by another brief narrative, such as, "The charts above show that the number of mathematics assessments including student writing has increased significantly in the past three years. Those assessments have emphasized the problem-solving portions of the state tests. The charts also show a strong increase in interdisciplinary mathematics instruction, with the frequency of math instruction in music, art, physical education, technology, science, and social studies much greater for the most recent school year than was the case in earlier years."

Right Panel: Includes inferences and conclusions, such as, "Our analysis of the data suggests that multidisciplinary instruction in math and writing in math have both been effective strategies to improve student performance. Therefore, we have planned to expand these strategies in the following ways: [examples of the strategies specifically applicable to the individual school]. We remain very concerned about the 16 percent of students who are not proficient on the math portion of the state tests and have developed individualized learning plans for each of these students. In addition, we have added the following intervention strategies for all nonproficient students: [specific strategies applicable to your school]."

Other Notes to Prepare for the "Science Fair for Grown-Ups":
1. Principals will not make formal presentations—the Data Walls speak for themselves. Principals should be prepared to respond to questions from colleagues about their Data Walls.

2. The primary function of the Data Wall and Science Fair is to allow principals to ask one another questions and share with one another informally how they achieved their successes. If the Science Fair takes place during a multiday leadership conference, then the displays should be set up during the breakfast of the first day and left up throughout the conference.

3. The process of continuous collaboration must continue all year, not just at the retreat. The Data Walls can be the focus of internal staff development, joint faculty meetings with other schools, and planning for instructional interventions and professional development activities.

4. CRITICALLY IMPORTANT: The Data Walls are not for the purpose of impressing outside observers, the superintendent, or any other external audience. The primary purpose of the Data Walls is for principals to share information with their fellow principals and, most important, with their faculties.

5. Principals will have to make choices regarding which data to use. They will want to show the information that is most important, drawing clear conclusions and making the point to the faculty members that they are not merely displaying data, but *using* data to inform their leadership decision making.

APPENDIX I

SCIENCE FAIR REFLECTIONS

The Treasure Hunt

Name: _____

Date: _____

1. Identify one or two important challenges that you face with regard to improving student achievement and educational equity.

| |
| |
| |
| |

2. Find one or two other displays that have a similar challenge with one of your challenges, but that appeared to have better results.

What did you notice that was *similar* in the strategies that were used on the other displays?

| |
| |
| |
| |

What did you notice that was *different* in the strategies that were used on the other displays?

| |
| |
| |
| |

What did you notice about the **results**? How are the results related to the strategies?

3. Data analysis and displays:

What did you notice about the data display that you can use to improve your displays for the next Science Fair? Identify two or three specific best practices in the display and communication of information.

4. Action plan:

Based on what you have learned during this Science Fair, what are your most important priorities with regard to refining strategies, communicating information, and achieving results?

5. Recommended improvements:

How can the next version of the Science Fair be improved in order to make this event most useful for you and the schools that you serve?

Your feedback and reflections are very important. Please turn in one complete copy of this form before you leave today. Thank you!

Copyright © 2007, the Leadership and Learning Center, (866) 399-6019.

References

Achilles, C. M. (1999). *Let's put kids first, finally: Getting class size right.* Thousand Oaks, CA: Corwin Press.

Ackerman, R. H., & Mackenzie, S. V. (2007). *Uncovering teacher leadership: Essays and voices from the field.* Thousand Oaks, CA: Corwin Press.

Ainsworth, L., & Christinson, J. (2007). *Five easy steps to a balanced math program for secondary teachers.* Englewood, CO: Advanced Learning Press.

Ainsworth, L., & Viegut, D. (2006). *Common formative assessments: How to connect standards-based instruction and assessment.* Thousand Oaks, CA: Corwin Press.

Barabási, A.-L. (2003). *Linked: How everything is connected to everything else and what it means.* New York: Plume.

Beck, M. (2006). *The four-day win: How to end your diet war and achieve thinner peace four days at a time.* New York: Simon & Schuster.

Bossidy, L., & Charan, R. (2004). *Confronting reality: Doing what matters to get things right.* New York: Crown Business.

Boyatzis, R. E., & McKee, A. (2005). *Resonant leadership: Renewing yourself and connecting with others through mindfulness, hope, and compassion.* Boston: Harvard Business School Press.

Brewster, C., & Fager, J. (2000, October). *Increasing student engagement and motivation: From time-on-task to homework.* Portland, OR: Northwest Regional Educational Laboratory. Retrieved July 18, 2007, from http://www.nwrel.org/request/oct00/cloak/ByRequest.pdf

Calkins, L. M. (1994). *The art of teaching writing* (2nd ed.). Portsmouth, NH: Heinemann.

Capella, E., & Weinstein, R. S. (2001, December). Turning around reading achievement: Predictors of high school students' academic resilience. *Journal of Educational Psychology, 93*(4), 758–771.

Carter, S. (1999). *No excuses: Seven principals of low-income schools who set the standard for high achievement.* Washington, DC: Heritage Foundation.

Chappuis, S., Stiggins, R., Arter, J., & Chappuis, J. (2004). *Assessment for learning: An action guide for school leaders* (2nd ed.). Princeton, NJ: Educational Testing Service.

Childress, S., Elmore, R., & Grossman, A. (2006, November). How to manage urban school districts. *Harvard Business Review, 84*(11), 130–138.

Coleman, J. (1966). *Equality of educational opportunity.* Washington, DC: U.S. Government Printing Office.

Collins, J. (2001). *Good to great: Why some companies make the leap . . . and others don't.* New York: HarperCollins.

Concise Oxford dictionary (10th ed.). (2001). Oxford, England: Oxford University Press.

Danielson, C. (2006). *Teacher leadership that strengthens professional practice.* Alexandria, VA: Association for Supervision and Curriculum Development.

Davis, S., Darling-Hammond, L., LaPointe, M., & Meyerson, D. (2005). *School leadership study: Developing successful principals.* Stanford, CA: Stanford University, Stanford Educational Leadership Institute.

DuFour, R., DuFour, R., Eaker, R., & Karhanek, G. (2004). *Whatever it takes: How professional learning communities respond when kids don't learn.* Bloomington, IN: National Educational Service.

Durrant, J., & Holden, G. (2005). *Teachers leading change: Doing research for school improvement* (Leading teachers, leading schools series). London: Paul Chapman.

Edmonds, R. R. (1979). Effective schools for the urban poor. *Educational Leadership, 37*(1), 15–24.

Elmore, R. (2000). *Building a new structure for school leadership.* Washington, DC: Albert Shanker Institute.

Fernandez, K. E. (2006). *Clark County School District study of the effectiveness of school improvement plans (SESIP).* (Tech. Rep.). Las Vegas, NV: Clark County School District.

Fink, D. (2005). *Leadership for mortals: Developing and sustaining leaders of learning* (Leading teachers, leading schools series). London: Paul Chapman.

Fuhrman, S. H., & Elmore, R. F. (2004). *Redesigning accountability systems for education.* New York: Teachers College Press.

Gladwell, M. (2002). *The tipping point: How little things can make a big difference.* Boston: Back Bay Books.

Goleman, D. (2006). *Social intelligence: The new science of human relationships.* New York: Bantam Books.

Goodlad, J. I. (1984). *A place called school: Prospects for the future.* New York: McGraw-Hill.

Green, J. L., Camilli, G., & Elmore, P. B. (Eds.). (2006). *Handbook of complementary methods in education research* (3rd ed.). Mahwah, NJ: Lawrence Erlbaum.

Guskey, T. R. (2000). *Evaluating professional development.* Thousand Oaks, CA: Corwin Press.

Guskey, T. R. (2002). *How's my kid doing? A parent's guide to grades, marks, and report cards.* San Francisco: Jossey-Bass.

Guskey, T. R. (Ed.). (2005). *Benjamin S. Bloom: Portraits of an educator.* Lanham, MD: Rowman & Littlefield.

Guskey, T. R., & Bailey, J. M. (2001). *Developing grading and reporting systems for student learning.* Thousand Oaks, CA: Corwin Press.

Haycock, K. (1999). *Dispelling the myth: High-poverty schools exceeding expectations.* Washington, DC: Education Trust.

Haycock, K. (2001). *Dispelling the myth revisited.* Washington, DC: Education Trust.

Howard, J. (1995, Fall). You can't get there from here: The need for a new logic in education reform. *Daedalus: Journal of the American Academy of Arts and Sciences, 124*(4), 85–92.

Kim, W. C., & Mauborgne, R. (2004, October). Blue ocean strategy. *Harvard Business Review, 82*(10), 76–84.

Kouzes, J. M., & Posner, B. Z. (2003a). *Credibility: How leaders gain it and lose it, why people demand it.* San Francisco: Jossey-Bass.

Kouzes, J. M., & Posner, B. Z. (2003b). *The leadership challenge* (rev. ed.). San Francisco: Jossey-Bass.

Krovetz, M. L., & Arriaza, G. (2006). *Collaborative teacher leadership: How teachers can foster equitable schools.* Thousand Oaks, CA: Corwin Press.

Kübler-Ross, E. (1969). *On death and dying: What the dying have to teach doctors, teachers, nurses, and their own family members.* New York: Touchstone.

Leithwood, K., Louis, K. S., Anderson, S., & Wahlstrom, K. (2004, September). *How leadership influences student learning.* Retrieved July 13, 2005, from http://www.wallacefoundation.org/WF/KnowledgeCenter/KnowledgeTopics/Education Leadership/HowLeadershipInfluencesStudentLearning.htm

Leonard, D., & Swap, W. (2005). *When sparks fly: Harnessing the power of group creativity.* Boston: Harvard Business School Publishing.

Levine, M. (2005). *Ready or not, here life comes.* New York: Simon & Schuster.

Marzano, R. J. (2006). *Classroom assessment and grading that work.* Alexandria, VA: Association for Supervision and Curriculum Development.

Marzano, R. J., Waters, T., & McNulty, B. A. (2005). *School leadership that works: From research to results.* Alexandria, VA: Association for Supervision and Curriculum Development.

McCourt, F. (2005). *Teacher man: A memoir.* New York: Scribner.

Merideth, E. M. (2006). *Leadership strategies for teachers.* Thousand Oaks, CA: Corwin Press.

Merriam-Webster online dictionary. (2007). Springfield, MA: Merriam-Webster. Available: http://www.m-w.com

Milgram, S. (1967, May). The small world problem. *Psychology Today, 1,* 60–67.

Moller, G., & Pankake, A. (2006). *Lead with me: A principal's guide to teacher leadership.* Larchmont, NY: Eye on Education.

Murphy, J. F. (2005). *Connecting teacher leadership and school improvement.* Thousand Oaks, CA: Corwin Press.

Peters, T. (2003). *Re-imagine! Business excellence in a disruptive age.* London: Dorling Kindersley.

Popham, W. J. (2006, November). Phony formative assessments: Buyer beware! *Educational Leadership, 64*(4), 86–87.

Putnam, R. D. (2000). *Bowling alone: The collapse and revival of American community.* New York: Simon & Schuster.

Rath, T., & Clifton, D. O. (2004). *How full is your bucket?: Positive strategies for work and life.* New York: Gallup Press.

Reeves, D. B. (2002). Galileo's dilemma: The illusion of scientific certainty in educational research. *Education Week, 21*(34), 33, 44.

Reeves, D. B. (2004a). *Accountability for learning: How teachers and school leaders can take charge.* Alexandria, VA: Association for Supervision and Curriculum Development.

Reeves, D. B. (2004b). *Accountability in action: A blueprint for learning organizations* (2nd ed.). Englewood, CO: Advanced Learning Press.

Reeves, D. B. (2004c). *Assessing educational leaders: Evaluating performance for improved individual and organizational results.* Thousand Oaks, CA: Corwin Press.

Reeves, D. B. (2004d). The case against zero. *Phi Delta Kappan, 86*(4), 324–325.

Reeves, D. B. (2005, April 3). *The multiple intelligences of leadership: An alternative vision of leadership effectiveness.* Presented at the 2005 Annual Conference of the Association for Supervision and Curriculum Development, Orlando, Florida.

Reeves, D. B. (2006a). *The learning leader: How to focus school improvement for better results.* Alexandria, VA: Association for Supervision and Curriculum Development.

Reeves, D. B. (2006b). Of hubs, bridges, and networks. *Educational Leadership, 63*(8), 32–37.

Reeves, D. B. (2007a, April 14). *Raising leaders: How to create a new generation of student leaders in every school and every neighborhood.* Unpublished keynote presentation at the meeting of the National School Boards Association, San Francisco, California.

Reeves, D. B. (2007b). Teachers step up. *Educational Leadership, 65*(1), 87–88.

Rosenthal, R., & Jacobson, L. (1968). *Pygmalion in the classroom: Teacher expectation and pupils' intellectual development.* New York: Holt, Rinehart & Winston.

Rosenthal, R., & Jacobson, L. (2003). *Pygmalion in the classroom: Teacher expectation and pupils' intellectual development.* Carmarthen: Crown House.

Rothstein, A. (2006, February 8). Students as coaches: One high school's experiment in using students' perceptions to help teachers improve instruction. *Education Week, 25*(22), 31–32.

Rothstein, R. (2004a). *Class and schools: Using social, economic, and educational reform to close the black-white achievement gap.* Washington, DC: Economic Policy Institute.

Rothstein, R. (2004b). Class and the classroom: Even the best schools can't close the race achievement gap. *American School Board Journal, 191*(10), 16.

Samuel-Stover, C. (2006). *From the inside out: How to transform your school to increase student achievement: A guide for principals, aspiring principals, and teacher leaders.* Charleston, SC: BookSurge.

Schmoker, M. J. (1999). *Results: The key to continuous school improvement* (2nd ed.). Alexandria, VA: Association for Supervision and Curriculum Development.

Schmoker, M. J. (2001). *The results fieldbook: Practical strategies from dramatically improved schools.* Alexandria, VA: Association for Supervision and Curriculum Development.

Schmoker, M. (2006). *Results now: How we can achieve unprecedented improvements in teaching and learning.* Alexandria, VA: Association for Supervision and Curriculum Development.

Shaughnessy, M. F. (2004, June). An interview with Anita Woolfolk: The educational psychology of teacher efficacy. *Educational Psychology Review, 16*(2), 153–176.

Sparks, D., & Hirsch, S. (1997). *A new vision for staff development.* Alexandria, VA, and Osford, OH: Association for Supervision and Curriculum Development and National Staff Development Council.

Stone, R., & Cuper, P. H. (2006). *Best practices for teacher leadership: What award-winning teachers do for their professional learning communities.* Thousand Oaks, CA: Corwin Press.

Tapscott, D., & Williams, A. D. (2006). *Wikinomics: How mass collaboration changes everything.* New York: Portfolio.

Thomas B. Fordham Institute and the Broad Foundation. (2003). *Better leaders for America's schools: A manifesto.* Retrieved July 24, 2007, from http://www.edexcellence.net/doc/manifesto.pdf

Tobacco Documents Online. (1977). *The arguments at our disposal.* In Anne Landman's collection. Retrieved July 24, 2007, from http://tobaccodocuments.org/landman/500084474-4486.html

Training today: R-E-S-P-E-C-T. (2006, June 1). *Training Magazine,* 12. Retrieved September 27, 2007, from http://www.allbusiness.com/services/educational-services/4285786-1.html

U.S. Department of Education. (2002). What Works Clearinghouse. Washington, DC: U.S. Department of Education, Institute of Education Sciences. Retrieved July 24, 2007, from http://ies.ed.gov/ncee/wwc/

Wilmore, E. L. (2007). *Teacher leadership: Improving teaching and learning from inside the classroom.* Thousand Oaks, CA: Corwin Press.

Wolk, R. (2007, June 20). Education research could improve schools, but probably won't. *Education Week, 26*(42), 38–39.

Woods, P. (2005). *Democratic leadership in education* (*Leading teachers, leading schools* series). London: Paul Chapman.

Zalesnik, A. (1977). Managers and leaders: Are they different? *Harvard Business Review, 55*(3), 67–78.

INDEX

Page numbers followed by *f* denote illustrations.

ABOUT THE AUTHOR

Douglas B. Reeves is the founder of the Leadership and Learning Center. He has worked with education, business, nonprofit, and government organizations throughout the world. The author of more than 20 books and many articles on leadership and organizational effectiveness, he has twice been named to the Harvard University Distinguished Authors Series. His monthly column on change leadership appears in *Educational Leadership*. Dr. Reeves was named the Brock International Laureate for his contributions to education. He also received the Distinguished Service Award from the National Association of Secondary School Principals and the Parents' Choice Award for his writing for children and parents. Free downloads of research, presentations, and articles by Dr. Reeves are available at www.LeadandLearn.com. He can be reached at DReeves@LeadandLearn.com or (978) 740-3001.

Related ASCD Resources:
Teacher Leadership and School Reform

Multimedia

Guide for Instructional Leaders, Guide 1: An ASCD Action Tool (#506138)

Guide for Instructional Leaders, Guide 2: An ASCD Action Tool by Grant Wiggins, John L. Brown, and Ken O'Connor (#703105)

Guide for Instructional Leaders, Guide 3: An ASCD Action Tool by Robby Champion, Anne Meek, and Karen M. Dyer (#703111)

Guiding School Improvement with Action Research Books-in-Action Package (10 Books and 1 video) (#700261)

Making School Improvement Happen with What Works in Schools: An ASCD Action Tool Set (Three Tools) by John L. Brown (#705055)

Networks

Visit the ASCD Web site (www.ascd.org) and click on About ASCD. Go to the section on Networks for information about professional educators who have formed groups around topics such as "Restructuring Schools." Look in the Network Directory for current facilitators' addresses and phone numbers.

Online Courses

Visit the ASCD Web site (www.ascd.org) for the following professional development opportunities:

Contemporary School Leadership by Vera Blake (#PD04OC38)

Creating and Sustaining Professional Learning Communities by Vera Blake and Diane Jackson (#PD04OC43)

What Works in Schools: An Introduction by John Brown (#PD04OC36)

Print Products

Accountability for Learning: How Teachers and School Leaders Can Take Charge by Douglas B. Reeves (#104004)

Align the Design: A Blueprint for School Improvement by Nancy J. Mooney and Ann T. Mausbach (#108005)

Educational Leadership, September 2007: Teachers as Leaders (#108020)

Educational Leadership, May 2006: Challenging the Status Quo (#106043)

Enhancing Professional Practice: A Framework for Teaching (2nd ed.) by Charlotte Danielson (#106034)

Enhancing Student Achievement: A Framework for School Improvement by Charlotte Danielson (#102109)

How to Thrive as a Teacher Leader by John G. Gabriel (#104150)

Leadership Capacity for Lasting School Improvement by Linda Lambert (#102283)

Leadership for Learning: How to Help Teachers Succeed by Carl D. Glickman (#101031)

The Learning Leader: How to Focus School Improvement for Better Results by Douglas B. Reeves (#105151)

Results Now: How We Can Achieve Unprecedented Improvements in Teaching and Learning by Mike Schmoker (#106045)

Teacher Leadership That Strengthens Professional Practice by Charlotte Danielson (#105048)

Video and DVD

Improving Instruction through Observation and Feedback (Three videos with a Facilitator's Guide) (#402058)

What Works in Schools (Three programs on DVD with a 140-page Facilitator's Guide) (#603047)

For more information, visit us on the World Wide Web (http://www.ascd.org); send an e-mail message to member@ascd.org; call the ASCD Service Center (1-800-933-ASCD or 703-578-9600, then press 2); send a fax to 703-575-5400; or write to Information Services, ASCD, 1703 N. Beauregard St., Alexandria, VA 22311-1714 USA.